The Gospel In Brief

LYOF N. TOLSTOI

AVENS FLOWER

Avensblume Press
1815 S. Saginaw Road
Midland, MI 48640

Published by Avensblume Press,
1815 South Saginaw Road,
Midland, Michigan 48640, U.S.A.

"Library of Congress Catalog Card Number."
92-075771

ISBN number 0-9634591-3-9

Original Copyright, 1899,
By THOMAS Y. CROWELL & CO.

Publisher's Cataloging in Publication
(Prepared by Quality Books Inc.)

Tolstoy, Leo, graf, 1828-1910.
    [Selections. English. 1993]
    The gospel in brief / Lyof N. Tolstoy. —2nd ed.
    p. cm.
    Translation from Russian.
    Includes index.
    ISBN 0-9634591-3-9

    1. Tolstoy, Leo, graf, 1828-1910—Religion. 2. Bible. N.T.
Gospels—Paraphrases, English. I. Title.

BS2555.T6452213 1993   2226'.06
                                        QBI93-20122

COUNT TOLSTOÏ

ORIGINAL SKETCH FROM LIFE BY RYEPIN

CONTENTS

AUTHOR'S PREFACE

THIS present book is extracted from a larger work, which exists in manuscript, and cannot be published in Russia.

That work consists of four parts, namely : —

1. An account of that course of my personal life, and of my thoughts, which led me to the conviction that in the Christian teaching lies the truth.

2. An investigation of the Christian teaching — first, according to the interpretation of the Greek Church solely ; then, according to the interpretation of the Churches generally, and the interpretation of the apostles, councils, and so-called " Fathers." Also, an exposition of the falsity in these interpretations.

An investigation of the Christian teaching, based, not upon the above interpretations, but solely upon the words and deeds ascribed to Christ by the four Gospels.

4. An exposition of the real meaning of the Christian teaching, of the motives for its perversions, and of the consequences to which it should lead.

From the third of these parts this present volume is condensed. I have there effected the fusion of the four Gospels into one, according to the real sense of the teaching. I had no need to digress from the order in which each Gospel is written, so that in my harmonisation the transpositions of verses, rather than being more, are less numerous than in the greater part of those known to me, and in our Grechoulevitch's version of the four Gospels. In my treatment of the Gospel of John there is no transposition, but all stands in the same order as in the original.

My division of the Gospel into twelve chapters (or six, since each pair of the twelve may be taken as one)

281

came about spontaneously from the nature of the teaching. The following is the purport of the chapters : —

1. Man is the son of the Infinite Source of Being; he is the son of this Father, not by the flesh but by the spirit.

2. And therefore, man must serve the Source of his being, in the spirit.

3. The life of all men has a divine Origin. This Origin only is sacred.

4. And therefore, man must serve this Source of all human life. This is the will of the Father.

5. Service of the Will of the Father of Life is life-giving.

6. And therefore, it is not necessary to life that each man should satisfy his own will.

7. This present life in time is the food of the true life.

8. And therefore, the true life is outside time; it is in the present.

9. Time is an illusion in life; the life of the past and the future clouds men from the true life of the present.

10. And therefore, one must aim to destroy the deception arising from the past and future, the life in time.

11. The true life is that now present to us, common to all, and manifesting itself in love.

12. And therefore, he who lives by love now, in this present, becomes, through the common life of all men, at one with the Father, the source, the foundation of life.

So that the chapters, in pairs, are related as cause and effect.

Besides these twelve chapters, this exposition includes — (*a*) The introduction of the first chapter of the Gospel of John, where the writer of the Gospel speaks, in his own name, as to the purport of the whole teaching : and (*b*) a portion of the same writer's Epistle (written probably before the Gospel); this containing the general sense to be derived from the preceding exposition.

These two parts are not essential to the teaching. Although the former, as well as the latter of them, might be omitted without loss (the more so as they come in the name of John, and not of Christ), I have, nevertheless, kept them, because, to a straightforward understanding of the whole teaching, these parts, confirming each other and the whole, as against the strange commentaries of the Churches, yield the plainest evidence of the meaning to be put upon the teaching.

At the beginning of each chapter, besides a brief indication of the subject, I had put words from the prayer taught by Jesus to His disciples, such as corresponded with the contents of the chapter.

At the conclusion of my work I found, to my astonishment and joy, that the Lord's Prayer is nothing less than Christ's whole teaching, stated in most concise form, and in that same order in which I had already arranged the chapters, each phrase of the prayer corresponding to the purport and sequence of the chapters, as follows: —

1. Our Father,	Man is the son of the Father.
2. Which art in heaven,	God is the infinite spiritual source of life.
3. Hallowed be Thy name,	May the Source of Life be held holy.
4. Thy kingdom come,	May His power be established over all men.
5. Thy will be done, as in heaven,	May His will be fulfilled, as it is in Himself,
6. So also on earth.	So also in the bodily life.
7. Give us our daily bread	The temporal life is the food of the true life.
8. This day.	The true life is in the present.
9. And forgive us our debts as we forgive our debtors,	May the faults and errors of the past not hide this true life from us,
10. And lead us not into temptation,	And may they not lead us into delusion,
11. But deliver us from evil,	So that no evil may come to us,
12. For Thine is the kingdom, the power, and the glory.	And there shall be order, and strength, and reason.

In that large third part from which this work is condensed, the Gospel according to the four Evangelists

is presented in full.   But in the rendering now given,
all passages are omitted which treat of the following
matters, namely, — John the Baptist's conception and
birth, his imprisonment and death; Christ's birth, and
his genealogy; his mother's flight with him into Egypt;
his miracles at Cana and Capernaum; the casting out
of devils; the walking on the sea; the cursing of the
fig-tree; the healing of sick, and the raising of dead
people; the resurrection of Christ Himself; and, finally,
the reference to prophecies fulfilled in His life.

These passages are omitted in this abridgment, because, containing nothing of the teaching, and describ-
ing only events which passed before, during, or after
the period in which Jesus taught, they complicate the
exposition.   However one takes them, under any cir-
cumstance, they bring to the teaching of Jesus neither
contradiction nor confirmation of its truth.   Their sole
significance for Christianity was that they proved the
divinity of Jesus Christ for him who was not persuaded
of this divinity beforehand.   But they are useless to
one whom stories of miracles are powerless to convince,
and who, besides, doubts the divinity of Jesus as evi-
denced in His teaching.

In the large work, every departure from the ordinary
version, as well as every comment added to the text,
and every omission, is made clear, and proved by the
comparison of the various versions of the Gospels, from
the examination of contexts, and finally, by consider-
ations, philological and other.   But in the present
abridged rendering, all these arguments and refutations
of the false understanding of the Churches, as well as
the minute notes and quotations, are omitted; because,
however true and exact they may be in their places,
they cannot carry conviction as to the true understanding of the teaching.   The justness of a conception
of this kind is better proved, not by arguing particular
points, but by its own unity, clearness, simplicity, full-
ness, as well as by its harmony with the inner feelings
of all who seek truth.   Speaking generally, in regard
to what divergence there is between my rendering and

the Church's authorized text, the reader must not for
get that it is a gross error to represent the four Gospels,
as is often done, to be books sacred in every verse and
in every syllable. The reader must not forget that
Jesus never Himself wrote a book, as did, for instance,
Plato, Philo, or Marcus Aurelius ; that He, moreover,
did not, as Socrates did, transmit His teaching to in-
formed and literate men, but spoke to a crowd of illiter-
ate men ; and that only a long time after His death men
began to write down what they had heard from Him.

The reader must not forget that a great number of
such accounts have been written, from which, at first,
the Churches selected three, and then another. Moreover, in selecting those which seemed to them the best
according to the proverb, " No stick without knots," the
Churches, out of the enormous heap of the Christian liter-
ature, have been forced to take in with their bargain a
great many knots ; so that the canonical Gospels contain
nearly as many faulty passages as those Gospels re-
jected as apocryphal.

The reader must not forget that it is the teaching of
Christ which may be sacred, but in no way can a certain
measure of verses and syllables be so ; and that certain
verses, from here to here, say, cannot be sacred merely
because men say they are so.

Moreover, the reader must not forget that these selected Gospels are, at any rate, the work of thousands of
various brains and hands of men ; that during centuries
the Gospels have been selected, enlarged, and com-
mented upon ; that the most ancient copies which have
come down to us, from the fourth century, are written
straight on without punctuation, so that, even after the
fourth and fifth centuries, they have been the subject
of the most diverse readings; and that such variations
in the Gospels may be counted up to fifty thousand.
The reader must have all this present in mind in order
to disengage himself from the opinion, so common
among us, that the Gospels, in their present shape, have
come to us directly from the Holy Spirit. The reader
must not forget that, far from it being blamable to dis

encumber the Gospels of useless passages, and to illumi
nate passages the one by the other, it is, on the contrary,
unreasonable not to do this, and to hold a certain number
of verses and syllables as sacred.

On the other hand, I pray my readers to remember
that, if I do not hold the Gospels to be sacred books
emanating from the Holy Spirit, I yet less regard the
Gospels as mere historical monuments of religious litera-
ture. I understand the theological as well as the historical standpoint on the Gospels, but regard the books
myself from quite another. I pray the readers of my
rendering not to be misled, either by the theological
view, or by that other, so usual in our day among educated men, the historical view, neither of which I hold
with. I consider Christianity to be neither a pure revelation nor a phase of history, but I consider it as the
only doctrine which gives a meaning to life.

And it is neither theology nor history which has won
me to Christianity; but just this, that, when fifty years
old, having questioned myself, and having questioned
the reputed philosophers whom I knew, as to what I
am, and as to the purport of my life, and after getting
the reply that I was a fortuitous concatenation of atoms,
and that my life was void of purport, and that life itself
is evil, I became desperate, and wished to put an end
to my life. But after recalling to myself how formerly, in
childhood, while I still had religious faith, life possessed
meaning for me; and that the great mass of men about
me, who hold to faith and are uncorrupted by wealth,
possess the meaning of life: after all this, I was brought
into doubt as to the justness of the reply given to me by
the wisdom of men of my own station, and I tried once
more to understand what answer it is that Christianity
gives to those men who live a life with meaning. And
I embarked upon the study of Christianity, as to what
in this teaching guides the lives of men. I began to
study that Christianity which I saw applied in life, and
to make the comparison of this applied Christianity with
the sources whence it percolates. The source of the
Christian teaching is the Gospels, and there I found the

explanation of the spirit which animates the life of all
who really live. But along with the flow of that pure,
life-giving water I perceived much mire and slime un-
rightfully mingled therewith ; and this had prevented
me, so far, from seeing the real, pure water. I found
that, along with the lofty Christian teaching, are bound
up the teachings of Hebraism and the Church, both of
which are repugnant and foreign to the former. I thus
felt myself in the position of a man to whom is given a
sack of refuse, who, after long struggle and wearisome
labor, discovers among the refuse a number of infinitely
precious pearls. This man then knows that he is not
blameworthy in his distaste for the dirt, and also that
those who have gathered these pearls at the same time
with the rest of the sackful, and who have preserved
them, are no more to blame than himself, but, on the
contrary, deserve love and respect.

I knew not the light, and I thought there was no
sure truth in life ; but when I perceived that only light
enables men to live, I sought to find the sources of the
light. And I found them in the Gospels, despite the
false commentaries of the Churches. And when I
reached this source of light I was dazzled with its
splendor, and I found there full answers to my ques-
tions as to the purport of the lives of myself and others,
— answers which I recognized as wholly harmonious
with all the known answers gained among other nations,
and, to my mind, surpassing all other answers.

I sought a solution of the problem of life, and not of
a theological or historical question ; and that is why I
was indifferent to know whether Jesus Christ is or is
not God, and from whom proceeds the Holy Spirit, etc.
And it is just as unimportant and unnecessary to know
when and by whom such and such a Gospel was written,
and whether such and such a parable came from Jesus
Himself or not. For me, the only important concern
was this light, which, for eighteen hundred years, has
shone upon mankind ; which has shone upon me likewise, and which shines upon me still. But to know,
more than this, how I ought to name the source of this

light, what elements compose it, and what kindled it, 1
in no way concerned myself.

I might end this preface here if the Gospels were
newly discovered books, and if the teaching of Jesus
had not been, these eighteen hundred years, the subject
of a continuous series of false interpretations. But to-
day, to rightly understand the teaching of Jesus as He
must needs have understood it Himself, it is indispensa-
ble to know the chief causes of these false interpretations. The prime cause of such false interpretations,
which make it now so difficult for us to recover the true
teaching of Jesus, is the fact that, under the cover of
the Christian teaching, have been preached the teachings of the Church, which are made up from explana-
tions of most contradictory writings, in which only a
small part of the true teaching enters; even that being
distorted, and adapted to the commentaries. The teaching of Christ, according to this misinterpretation, is simply one link in the great chain of revelation which began
with the world's beginning, and stretches into the Church
of our own time.

These misinterpreters call Jesus God; but the recognition of His divinity does not make them recognize a
greater importance in His words and teaching than in
the words of the Pentateuch, the Psalms, the Acts, the
Epistles, the Apocalypse, or even the decisions of the
Councils and the writings of the Fathers.

And this false understanding allows no presentment
of the teaching of Jesus which does not accord with the
revelations which have preceded and followed Him;
doing this with the purpose, not to make clear the meaning of the teaching of Jesus, but to harmonize, as far as
possible, various writings which contradict each other;
such as the Pentateuch, the Psalms, the Gospels, Epistles, Acts, and, generally, all those which pass for
sacred.

It is possible, indeed, to make a limitless number of
such interpretations, having for object, not truth, but
the reconcilement of those two irreconcilables, the Old
and the New Testaments. And, in fact, the number of

these is unlimited. This is the case with the Epistles of Paul, and with the decisions of the Councils (which last begin with the formula: "It is the will of us and the Holy Spirit"); and such, also, is the case with the decrees of popes and synods, with the teachings of the Khlysty,[1] and with all false interpreters of the thought of Jesus. All recur to the same gross sanctions of the truth of their reconcilements, affirming that these reconcilements are not the result of their personal thought, but a direct witness from the Holy Spirit.

Without entering upon an analysis of these different dogmatic systems, each of which pretends to be the only true one, we may, nevertheless, well see that all of them, beginning by holding sacred the multitude of writings which make up the Old and New Testaments, thereby impose upon themselves an insurmountable barrier to the understanding of the real teaching of Jesus; and out of this confusion necessarily results the possibility, and even the necessity, of an infinite variety of opposed sects.

The reconcilement of all the revelations can be infinitely varied, but the explanation of the teaching of one person, and one looked upon as a God, should, on the contrary, not give rise to any difference of sect. It is impossible there should be conflicting ways of interpreting the teaching of a God come down to earth. If God had so come down to reveal unfailing truth to men, at least He would have revealed it in such a way that all might understand; if, then, this has not been done, that is because it was not God who came; or if, indeed, the truths of God are such that God Himself cannot make them plain to mankind, how can men do so?

If, on the other hand, Jesus was not God, but only a great man, His teaching can still less engender sects. For the teaching of a great man is only great because it explains in a clear, understandable way that which others have set out obscurely, incomprehensibly. That which is incomprehensible in the teaching of a great man is not great. The teaching of a great man can, there

---

[1] A Russian sect.

fore, engender no sects. Only, then, this interpretation, which pretends to be a revelation from the Holy Spirit, and to contain the sole truth, raises up antagonisms and gives birth to sects. However much the sects of various religions may assure us that they do not condemn those of other sects, that they pray for union with them, and have no hate to them, it is not true. Never, since the time of Arius, has a single dogma arisen from other cause than the desire to contradict an opposing dogma.

To maintain that a particular dogma is a divine revelation, inspired by the Holy Spirit, is in the highest degree presumption and folly. The highest presumption, because there is nothing more arrogant than for a man to say, "What I tell you, God Himself says through my mouth." And the highest folly, because there is nothing more stupid than to reply to one who says that God speaks by his mouth, "God says quite the opposite, and by mine own mouth." But in this way reason all the Churches; and hence have been born, and are now being born, all the sects and all the evil brought, and being brought, into the world in the name of religion.

And yet deeper than this surface evil, all the sects. cherish a second internal vice, which destroys in them any character of clearness, certainty, and honesty. It is this. While these sects present us with their false interpretations, as the last revelation from the Holy Spirit, they are careful never to precisely and decisively determine what is the very essence and purport of this revelation, which they profess is continued through them, and which they call "the Christian teaching."

All the sectarians who accept the revelation from the Holy Spirit, along with the Mohammedans, recognize Moses, Jesus, and Mohammed. The Churchmen accept Moses, Jesus, and the Holy Spirit. But to Mohammedanism, Mohammed is the last prophet, who alone has given the definite explanation of the two preceding revelations, — this is the last revelation, which explains all the preceding; and this one every true believer has before him.

With the religion of the Churches it is quite otherwise. That also, like the Mohammedan, accepts three revelations, but in place of calling their religion by the name of their last revealer, that is, the "religion of the Holy Spirit," they maintain their religion to be that of Jesus, and refer themselves to His teaching. So that, in giving to us what are really their own doctrines, they pretend to rest them upon the authority of Jesus.

Those religions of the Holy Spirit which offer to us the last and most decisive of revelations, whether it be in the writings of the Apostle Paul or the decisions of such and such Councils, or the decrees of popes or patriarchs, ought to say so, and call their faith by the name of him who had the last revelation. And if the last revelation is by the Fathers of the Church, or a decree of the Patriarch of the East, or a papal encyclical, or the syllabus or the catechism of Luther or Philaretus, people should say so, and call their faith by this name; because the last revelation, which explains all the preceding, is always the most important one. But they decline to adorn their dogmatic systems with the names of these authorities, and, continuing to preach quite against Christ's own teaching, they persist in maintaining that Jesus has revealed their doctrine to them. So that, according to their teaching, Jesus declared that He, by His blood, redeemed our humanity, ruined through Adam's sin; that there are three Persons in God; that the Holy Spirit came down upon the apostles, and was transmitted to the priesthood by the laying on of hands; that seven sacraments are necessary to salvation; that communion must be in two kinds; and so on. They would have us believe that all this is part of the teaching of Jesus; whereas we shall there seek in vain even the least allusion to any such matters. The Churches which so pretend would do well in concluding to give all this to us at once as the doctrine of the Holy Spirit, not of Jesus; for, in short, only those are Christians who hold the revelation of Jesus Himself as the decisive one, in virtue of His own saying, that His followers must own no other master than Himself.

It would seem that the matter is so plain that it is not worth thinking about; but however strange it seems to say so, it is none the less true that up till now the teaching of Jesus is not separated, on the one hand, from artificial and unwarrantable connection with the Old Testament, and, on the other hand, from the superadded fantastic notions which have been imposed upon it under cover of the name of the Holy Spirit. Up to now, there are some who, in calling Jesus the second Person of the Trinity, will not conceive of His teaching otherwise than as in accordance with the so-called revelations of the third Person, as these are found in the Old Testament, the decrees of Councils, and the conclusions of the Fathers of the Church; and in preaching the most extravagant things, they affirm these extravagances to be the religion of Christ. Others there are who, in refusing to regard Jesus as a God, similarly conceive of His teaching, not at all as He Himself declared it, but as what Paul and the other interpreters have made of it. Whilst considering Jesus as a man, and not as a God, these learned men deprive Him of a common natural right: the right of being held responsible for His own words only, and not for the words of His misinterpreters. In their endeavors to elucidate the teaching of Jesus, they attribute to Him ideas which He never thought of uttering. The representatives of this school, to begin with Renan, the most popular of them, do not see it their duty to take the trouble of distinguishing between that which bears the stamp of Jesus Himself and that which His interpreters have wrongly ascribed to Him. And, instead of thus troubling to search out the teaching of Jesus Himself a little more deeply than the Churches have done, they have been led to seek in the events of His life, and in the facts of history contemporary with Him, the explanation of His influence and of the diffusion of His ideas.

The problem they are called upon to solve is, in effect, this —

Eighteen hundred years ago a poor wanderer appeared on earth who taught certain things. He was flogged and executed. And since then, although many and many just men have suffered for the belief, millions of people, wise and foolish, learned and ignorant, cannot shake off the conviction that this man, alone among men, was God. Here is a strange phenomenon; how is it to be explained? The Churches explain it by saying that this man, Jesus, was really God, by which everything is explained. But if this man was not God, how are we to explain why this mere man, in particular, has been acknowledged as God?

On this point the learned people of our schools of history gather with extreme care every detail of the life of this man, without noticing that, even though they should succeed in gathering a great number of these details (in truth, they have gathered none); and even though they should succeed in entirely reconstructing the life of Jesus in the smallest details, the supreme question remains unanswered, — the question as to why Jesus, and no one else, exercised such an influence over men. The answer to this is not found in knowledge of the society in which Jesus was born, brought up, and so on; still less is it found in knowledge of the happenings in the Roman world at about this time, or in the fact that the people were inclined to superstitious beliefs. To gain this answer, it is only needful to find what precisely was the especial mark of Jesus which has led so many people to raise Him above the rest of men, and, for eighteen hundred years, to hold Him as a God.

He who would solve this problem, it would seem, must, before all, bring himself to understand the teaching of Jesus: His true teaching, clearly seen, and not the crude interpretations which have been put upon it. But this is just what is neglected. The learned historians of Christianity are so satisfied to think that Jesus was no God, they are so keen to prove that His teaching holds nothing divine, and is, therefore, not binding, that they are not alive to a very plain fact: they do not see that, the more they prove Jesus to have been simply a man, and in nothing divine, the darker and more insoluble they make the problem they have in hand. They are

making their full efforts to prove that He was simply a
man, that, therefore, His teaching is not obligatory. To
see clearly this astonishing error, one has only to remember the last writings of Renan's follower, M. Havet, who
remarks, with much simplicity, "Christ was never, in
anything, a Christian." And M. Soury, for his part, is
altogether ravished with the idea that Jesus was a cul-
tureless man, a simple soul.

The essential thing is : not to prove that Jesus was no
God, and His doctrine not divine, any more than to prove
He was not a Catholic : but to know what His teaching
essentially is ; that teaching which has seemed to men
so lofty and so precious, that they have again and again
owned Him for God who gave it to them.

If the reader belongs to that vast body of educated
men who have been brought up in the beliefs of a Church,
and who have not renounced its absurdities ; if he be a
man of reason and conscience (whether retaining love
and respect for the Christian teaching, or whether, following the proverb, "Burn the coat now the vermin
have got in," he thinks the whole of Christianity a per-
nicious superstition), I pray him to reflect that that which
shocks him, and seems to him a superstition, is not the
real teaching of Jesus ; and that it were unjust to make
Jesus responsible for the follies which have, since His
time, incrusted His teaching. It is only necessary to
study the teaching of Jesus in its proper form, as it has
come down to us in the words and deeds which are
recorded as His own. With readers of the kind I have
addressed, my book will go to show that Christianity is
not only a mixture of things sublime and things base ;
that it is not only not a superstition, but that, on the
contrary, it is the most convincing presentment of meta-
physics and morals, the purest and most complete doctrine of life, and the highest light which the human
mind has ever reached ; a doctrine from which all the
noblest activities of humanity in politics, science, poetry,
and philosophy instinctively derive themselves.

If, on the other hand, my reader belongs to that small
minority of educated men who remain attached to Church

doctrines, and who accept religion, not for an outward end, but to gain inward quietude, then I ask such a reader to remember that the teaching of Christ, as set forth herein, is quite other than that teaching as he has been given to understand it; and that, therefore, the question for him is, not as to whether the doctrine here put before him agrees with his beliefs, but, as to which is more in harmony with his reason and his heart — the teaching of his Church composed of reconcilèments of many scriptures, or the pure teaching of Jesus. It concerns him only to decide whether he will accept the new teaching, or whether he prefers to retain the teaching of his Church.

If, finally, my reader belongs to the category of men who value and accept outwardly the belief of some Church, not at all for truth's sake, but for the outward consideration of gains that come therefrom, such an one should inform himself that, whatever be the number of his coreligionists, whatever their power, whatever their station, even though monarchs, and whatever lofty personages they can reckon among them, he himself forms one of a party, not of the accusers, but of the accused. Such readers should inform themselves that they are not asked to furnish arguments for their case, because, this long while, all such arguments have been given which can be given; and even should they cite their proofs, they would only prove that which every one of the hundreds of opposing sects proves in its own case.

And, in truth, such people need not to prove anything, but to clear themselves, first, of the sacrilege they commit in putting the teaching of Jesus, whom they hold to be God, upon the same footing as the teachings of Ezra, of the Councils, of Theophylact; and in allowing themselves to distort the sayings of God into agreement with the sayings of men. Again, they must clear themselves of blasphemy in ascribing to God-Jesus all the zealotry which abides in their own hearts, and declaring it to be teaching of Christ. And finally, they must clear themselves of the treason they commit in hiding from men the teaching of God, who has come down to earth to bring us salvation; and by sliding in, to displace this teaching, the tradition of the Holy Spirit, thus depriving thousands of millions of that salvation which Jesus brought for men; and thus, instead of peace and love, bringing in all the diversity of sects, and all the recriminations, murders, and all sorts of misdeeds which follow.

For these readers there are only two issues: either to make humble submission, and renounce their deceits; or, to persecute those who arise to accuse them of the evil they have done and are doing.

If they will not renounce their deceits, it remains for them to take the only other part, that is, to persecute me. For which, in now completing my writing, I am prepared, with joy, and with fear for my own human weakness.

THE GOSPEL IN BRIEF

CHAPTER I

THE SON OF GOD

Man, the son of God, is powerless in the flesh, and free in the spirit

("Our Father")

Mt. i. 18. THE birth of Jesus Christ was thus:—
His mother Mary was betrothed to Jo
seph.   But, before they began to live as man
19. and wife, Mary proved with child.   But Joseph
was a good man, and did not wish to disgrace
24. her; he took her as his wife, and had nothing
25. to do with her until she had borne her first son,
and called him Jesus.

Lk. ii. 40.   And the boy grew and matured, and was
intelligent beyond his years.
41.   Jesus was twelve years old; and it happened
42. that Mary and Joseph went to the ·feast at
43. Jerusalem, and took the boy with them.   The
44. feast was over, and they went homeward, and
forgot about the boy.   Afterward they recol-
lected, and thought that he had gone off with
45. the children, and they inquired about him along
the road.   He was nowhere to be found, and
46. they went back to Jerusalem after him.   And
it was the third day before they found the boy
in the temple, sitting with the teachers, ques-
47. tioning them, and listening.   And every one
48. wondered at his intelligence.   His mother
caught sight of him, and said: "Why have

you done this way with us? Your father and
I have been grieving, and looking for you."
And he said to them: "But where did you   Lk.   ii. 49.
look for me? Surely you ought to know that
the son must be looked for in his Father's
house?" And they did not understand his   50.
words; they did not understand whom it was
he called his Father.

And after this, Jesus lived at his mother's,   51.
and obeyed her in everything. And he ad-   52.
vanced in age and intelligence. And every   iii. 23.
one thought that Jesus was the son of Joseph;
and so he lived to the age of thirty.

At that time the prophet John appeared in   Mt.   iii. 1.
Judea. He lived in the desert of Judea, on   Mk.   i. 4.
the Jordan. John's clothes were of camel's   Mt.   iii. 4.
hair, girt round the waist with a strap; and
he fed on bark and herbs.

He summoned the people to a change of   Mk.   i. 4.
life, in order to get rid of wickedness; and,
as a sign of the change of life, he bathed people in the Jordan. He said: "A voice calls   Lk.   iii. 4.
to you: Open a way for God through the wild
places, clear the way for Him. Make it so   5.
that all may be level, that there may be neither
hollows nor hills, neither high nor low. Then   6.
God will be among you, and all will find their
salvation."

And the people asked him, "What are we   10.
to do?" He answered: "Let him who has two   11.
suits of clothes give one to him who has none.
Let him who has food give to him who has
none." And tax-collectors came to him, and   12.
asked: "What are we to do?" He said to   13.
them: "Extort nothing beyond what is ordered." And soldiers asked: "How are we   14.
to live?" He said: "Do no one any harm,
do not deal falsely; be content with what is
served out to you."

And inhabitants of Jerusalem came to him,   Mt.   iii. 5.

and all the Jews in the neighborhood of the
Mt. iii. 6. Jordan. And they acknowledged their wickedness to him; and, in sign of the change of
life, he bathed them in the Jordan.

7. And many of the orthodox and conventional
religionists also came to John, but secretly. He
recognized them, and said : "You race of vipers!
Have you, also, got wind of it, that you cannot
8. escape the will of God? Then bethink yourselves, and change your faith! And if you
wish to change your faith, let it be seen by
your fruits that you have bethought yourselves.
10. The ax is already laid to the tree. If the
tree produces bad fruit, it will be cut down
11. and cast into the fire. In sign of your change
I cleanse you in water; but, along with this
bathing, you must be cleansed with the spirit.
12. The spirit will cleanse you, as a master cleanses
his threshing-floor; when he gathers the wheat,
but burns the chaff."

13. Jesus came from Galilee to the Jordan to be
bathed by John; and he bathed, and heard
John's preaching.
iv. 1. And from the Jordan he went into the wild
2. places, and there he strove in the spirit. Jesus
passed forty days and nights in the desert,
without food or drink.
Lk. iv. 3. And the voice of his flesh said to him : " If
you were Son of the Almighty God, you might
of your own will make loaves out of stones;
but you cannot do this, therefore you are not
4. Son of God." But Jesus said to himself : " If
I cannot make bread out of stones, this means
that I am not Son of a God of the flesh, but
Son of the God of the spirit. I am alive, not
by bread, but by the spirit. And my spirit is
able to disregard the flesh."

But hunger, nevertheless, tormented him;
and the voice of the flesh again said to him :
" If you live only by the spirit, and can disre

gard the flesh, then you can throw off the flesh,
and your spirit will remain alive." And it Lk. iv. 9.
seemed to him that he was standing on the
roof of the temple, and the voice of the flesh
said to him: "If you are Son of the God of
the spirit, throw yourself off the temple. You
will not be killed. But an unforeseen force will 10.
keep you, support you, and save you from all
harm." But Jesus said to himself: "I can 11.
12.
disregard the flesh, but may not throw it off,
because I was born by the spirit into the flesh.
This was the will of the Father of my spirit,
and I cannot oppose Him."

Then the voice of the flesh said to him: "If
you cannot oppose your Father by throwing
yourself off the temple and discarding life,
then you also cannot oppose your Father by
hungering when you need to eat. You must
not make light of the desires of the flesh; they
were placed in you, and you must serve them."
Then Jesus seemed to see all the kingdoms of 5.
the earth, and all mankind, just as they live
and labor for the flesh, expecting gain therefrom. And the voice of the flesh said to him: 6.
"Well, you see, these work for me, and I give
them all they wish for. If you will work for 7.
me you will have the same." But Jesus said 8.
to himself: "My Father is not flesh, but spirit.
I live by Him; I always know that He is in
me. Him alone I honor, and for Him alone I
work, expecting reward from Him alone."

Then the temptation ceased, and Jesus knew 13.
the power of the spirit.

And when he had known the power of the 14.
spirit, Jesus went out of the wild places, and Jn. i. 35.
went again to John, and stayed with him.

And when Jesus was leaving John, John said 36.
of him: "This is the saviour of men."

On account of these words of John, two of 37.
John's disciples left their former teacher and

Jn. i. 38. went after Jesus. Jesus, seeing them following him, stopped and said: "What do you
want?" They said to him: "Teacher! we
wish to be with you, and to know your teach-
39. ing." He said: "Come with me, and I will
tell you everything." They went with him,
and stayed with him, listening to him until the
tenth hour.

40. One of these disciples was called Andrew.
41. Andrew had a brother Simon. Having heard
Jesus, Andrew went to his brother Simon, and
said to him: "We have found him of whom
the prophets wrote, the Messiah; we have
found him who has announced to us our sal-
42. vation." Andrew took Simon with him, and
brought him also to Jesus. Jesus called this
brother of Andrew, Peter, which means a
stone. And both these brothers became disciples of Jesus.

43. Afterward, before entering Galilee, Jesus
met Philip, and called him to go with him.
44. Philip was from Bethsaida, and a fellow-vil-
45. lager of Peter and Andrew. When Philip
knew Jesus, he went and found his brother
Nathanael, and said to him: "We have found
the chosen of God, of whom the prophets and
Moses wrote. This is Jesus, the son of Joseph,
46. from Nazareth." Nathanael was astonished
that he of whom the prophets wrote should be
from the neighboring village, and said: "It
is most unlikely that the messenger of God
47. should be from Nazareth." Philip said: "Come
with me, you shall see and hear for yourself."
48. Nathanael agreed, and went with his brother,
and met Jesus; and, when he had heard him,
49. he said to Jesus: "Yes, now I see that this is
true, that you are the Son of God and the king
51. of Israel." Jesus said to him: "Learn something more important than that. Henceforth
heaven is opened, and people may be in com-

munion with the forces of heaven. Henceforth
God will be no longer separate from men."

And Jesus came home to Nazareth; and on
the Sabbath he went as usual into the synagogue, and began to read. They gave him the
book of the prophet Isaiah, and, unrolling it,
he began to read. In the book was written:—
"The spirit of the Lord is in me. He has
chosen me to announce happiness to the unfortunate and the broken-hearted, to announce
freedom to those who are bound, light to the
blind, and salvation and rest to the weary. To
announce to all men the time of God's mercy."

He folded the book, gave it to the attendant,
and sat down. And all waited to hear what
he should say. And he said: "This writing
has now been fulfilled before your eyes."

Lk. iv. 16.

17.

18.

19.

20.

CHAPTER II

LIFE IN THE SPIRIT

Therefore man must work, not for the flesh, but for the spirit

("Which art in heaven")

It happened once that Jesus, with his disciples, went through a field on the Sabbath.
His disciples were hungry, and on the way
plucked ears of corn, bruised them in their
hands, and ate the grain. But, according to
the teaching of the orthodox, God had made
an agreement with Moses, that all should observe the Sabbath, and do nothing on that day.
According to this teaching of the orthodox, God
commanded that he who worked on the Sabbath should be stoned to death. The orthodox
saw that the disciples were bruising ears of
corn on the Sabbath, and said; "It is not

Mt. xii. 1.
Mk. ii. 23.
Lk. vi. 1.

Mt. xii. 2

right to do so on the Sabbath. One must not
work on the Sabbath, and you are bruising
ears of corn. God ordained the Sabbath, and
commanded the breaking of it should be punished with death." Jesus heard this, and said:

Mt. xii. 7. "If you understand what is the meaning of
God's words, 'I desire love, and not sacrifice,'
you would not attach blame to that which is
8. not blameworthy. Man is more important than
the Sabbath."

Lk. xiii. 10. It happened another time, on a Sabbath, that
11. when Jesus was teaching in the synagogue, a
sick woman came up to him and asked him to
12-14. help her. And Jesus began to cure her. Then
the orthodox church-elder was angry with Jesus
for this, and said to the people: "It is said in
the law of God: There are six days in the week
xiv. 3. on which to work." But Jesus, in reply, asked
the orthodox professors of the law: "Well,
then, in your opinion, may not one help a man
6. on the Sabbath?" And they did not know
5. what to answer. Then Jesus said: "Deceiv-
Lk. xiii. 15. ers! Does not each of you untie his beast
from the manger and lead him to water on the
Mt. xii. 11. Sabbath? And if his sheep falls into a well,
any one will run and drag it out, although even
12. on the Sabbath. And a man is much better
than a sheep. But you say that one must not
Mk. iii. 4. help a man. What, then, in your opinion, must
one do on the Sabbath, good or evil: save a
soul or destroy it? Good must be done always,
on the Sabbath too."

Mt. ix. 9. Jesus once saw a tax-gatherer receiving taxes.
The tax-gatherer was called Matthew. Jesus
began to speak with him, and Matthew understood him, liked his teaching, and invited him
to his house, and showed him hospitality.
10. When Jesus came to Matthew, there came also
Matthew's friends, tax-gatherers and unbelievers, and Jesus did not disdain them, and sat

down, he and his disciples. And the orthodox saw this, and said to Jesus' disciples: "How is it that your teacher eats with tax-gatherers and unbelievers?" According to the teaching of the orthodox, God forbade communion with unbelievers. Jesus heard, and said: "He who is satisfied with his health does not need a doctor, but he who is ill, does. Understand what is the meaning of God's words: 'I desire love and not sacrifice.' I cannot teach a change of faith to those who consider themselves orthodox, but I teach those who consider themselves unbelievers."

There came to Jesus orthodox professors of the law from Jerusalem. And they saw that his disciples and Jesus himself ate bread with unwashed hands; and these orthodox began to condemn him for this, because they themselves strictly observed, according to church tradition, how plates and dishes should be washed, and would not eat unless they had been so washed. Also, they would eat nothing from the market unless they had washed it.

And the orthodox professors of the law asked him: "Why do you live not according to church tradition, but take and eat bread with unwashed hands?" And he answered them: "But in what way do you break God's commandment, following your church tradition? God said to you: 'Honor your father and mother.' But you have twisted it so that every one can say: 'I give to God what I used to give my parents.' And he who so says need not support his father and mother. Thus, then, you break God's commandment by church tradition. Deceivers! The prophet Isaiah spoke the truth about you: 'Because this people only fall down before me in words, and honor me with their tongue, while their heart is far from me; and because their fear of me is only a human law which

*Margin references:*

Mt. ix. 11

12.

13.

Mk. xv. 1.
Mk. vii. 1.
Mt. xv. 2.
Mk. vii. 2.

3.

4.

5.

Mt. xv. 3.

Mk. vii. 10, 11.

12.

13.

Mt. xv. 7.
8.

9

they have learnt by heart; therefore I will perform a wonderful, an extraordinary thing upon
this people: The wisdom of its wise men shall
be lost, and the reason of its thinkers shall be
dimmed. Woe to them who take thought to
hide their desires from the Eternal, and who
Mk. vii. 8. do their deeds in darkness.' And so it is with
you: You leave that which is important in the
law, that which is God's commandment, and
observe your human tradition as to the washing of cups!"

14. And Jesus called the people to him, and
15. said: "Hearken all, and understand: There
is nothing in the world that, entering a man,
could defile him; but that which goes forth
from him, this defiles a man. Let love and
mercy be in your soul, and then all will be
16. clean. Try to understand this."

17. And when he returned home, his disciples
18. asked him: "What do these words mean?"
And he said: "Do you also not understand
this? Do you not understand that everything
external, that which is of the flesh, cannot de-
19. file a man? The reason is, it enters not his
soul, but his body. It enters the body, and
20. afterward goes out from it. Only that can
defile a man which goes out from the man
21. himself, from his soul. Because from the soul
of man proceed evil, fornication, impurity, murder, theft, covetousness, wrath, deceit, insolence,
envy, calumny, pride, and every kind of folly.
23. All this evil is out of the soul of man and it
alone can defile a man."

Jn.   ii. 13. After this, the Passover came, and Jesus
went to Jerusalem, and entered the temple.
14. In the inclosure of the temple stood cattle,
cows, bulls, rams; and there were cotes full of
pigeons, and money-changers behind their
counters. All this was necessary in order to
make offerings to God. The animals were

slaughtered and offered in the temple. This was the method of prayer among the Jews, as taught by the orthodox professors of the law. Jesus went into the temple, twisted a whip, drove all the cattle out of the inclosure, and set free all the doves. And he scattered all the money, and bade that none of this should be brought into the temple. He said : " The prophet Isaiah said to you : The house of God is not the temple in Jerusalem, but the whole world of God's people. And the prophet Jeremiah also told you : Do not believe the falsehoods that here is the house of the Eternal. Do not believe this, but change your life ; do not judge falsely ; do not oppress the stranger, the widow, and the orphan ; do not shed innocent blood, and do not come into the house of God, and say : Now we may quietly do foul deeds. Do not make my house a den of robbers."

Jn. ii. 15

16.

Mt. xxi. 13.

Mk. xi. 17.
(Isa. lvi. 7.
Jer. vii. 4,
11.)

And the Jews began to dispute, and said to him : " You say that our piety is wrong. By what proofs will you show this ? " And, turning to them, Jesus said : " Destroy this temple and I will in three days awaken a new, living temple." And the Jews said : " But how will you at once make a new temple, when this was forty-six years in building ? " And Jesus said to them : " I speak to you of that which is more important than the temple. You would not say this if you understood the meaning of the words of the prophet : I, God, do not rejoice at your offerings, but rejoice at your love to each other. The living temple is the whole world of men, when they love each other."

18.

19.

20.

Mt. xii. 6.

7.

And then in Jerusalem many people believed in what he said. But he himself believed in nothing external, because he knew that everything is within man. He had no need that any one should give witness of man, because he knew that in man is the spirit.

Jn. ii. 23.

24.

25.

Jn. iv. 4. And Jesus happened once to be passing
5. through Samaria. He passed by the Samaritan
village of Sychar, near the place which Jacob
6. gave to his son Joseph. There was Jacob's
well. Jesus was tired, and sat beside the well.
8. His disciples went into the town to fetch bread.
7. And a woman came from Sychar to draw water,
9. and Jesus asked her to give him to drink. And
she said to him : " How is it that you ask me to
give you to drink ? For you Jews have no inter-
course with us Samaritans."
10. But he said to her : " If you knew me, and
knew what I teach, you would not say this, and
you would give me to drink, and I would give
13. you the water of life. Whoever drinks of the
14. water you have will thirst again. But whoever
shall drink of the water I have shall always be
satisfied, and this water shall bring him ever-
19. lasting life." The woman understood that he
was speaking of things divine, and said to him :
" I see that you are a prophet, and wish to teach
20. me. But how are you to teach me divine things,
when you are a Jew and I a Samaritan? Our
people worship God upon this hill, but you Jews
say that the house of God is only in Jerusalem.
You cannot teach me divine things, because you
have one belief, and we another." And Jesus
21. said to her : " Believe me, woman, the time is
already here, when people, to pray to the Father,
23. will come neither to this hill nor to Jerusalem.
The time has come when the real worshipers
of God will worship the Heavenly Father in
24. spirit and with works. Such are the worshipers the Father needs. God is a spirit, and He
must be worshiped in the spirit and with
25. works." The woman did not understand what
he told her, and said : I have heard that the
messenger of God will come, he whom they call
the anointed. He will then declare every-
26. thing." And Jesus said to her : " It is I, the

same who has spoken with you. Expect nothing more."

After this, Jesus came into the land of Judea, Jn. iii. 22
and there lived with his disciples, and taught.
At that time John taught the people near Salim, 23.
and bathed them in the river Enon. For John 24.
was not yet put in prison.

And a dispute arose between the disciples of 25.
John and the hearers of Jesus, as to which was
better, John's cleansing in water or Jesus' teaching. And they came to John, and said to him: 26
"You cleanse with water, but Jesus only teaches,
and all go to him. What have you to say of 27.
him?" John said: "A man of himself can
teach nothing, unless God teach him. Who 31.
speaks of the earth, is of the earth; but whosoever speaks of God, is from God. It is no- 32-34.
wise possible to prove whether the words that
are spoken are from God or not from God. God
is a spirit; He cannot be measured, and He
cannot be proved. He who shall understand
the word of the spirit, by this very thing proves
that he is of the spirit. The Father, loving His 35.
Son, has intrusted all to him. Whoever be- 36.
lieves in the Son has life, and whoever does not
believe in the Son has not life. God is the
spirit in man."

After this there came to Jesus one of the or- Lk. xi. 37.
thodox, and invited him to dinner. Jesus went
in and sat down at table. The host noticed that 38.
he did not wash before dinner, and wondered
thereat. And Jesus said to him: "You ortho- 39-41.
dox wash everything outside; but are you clean
inside? Be well-disposed to men, and all will
be clean."

And while he sat in the house of the orthodox, vii. 37.
there came a woman of the town, who was an
unbeliever. She had learnt that Jesus was in
the house of the orthodox man, and she came
there too, bringing a bottle of scent. And she 38

knelt at his feet, wept, and washed his feet with
her tears, wiped them with her hair, and poured
Lk. vii 39 scent over them. The orthodox man saw this,
and thought to himself: "He is hardly a prophet. If he were really a prophet, he would
know what kind of a woman it is that is washing his feet. He would know that this is a
wrong-doer, and would not allow her to touch
40. him." Jesus guessed his thought, and, turning
to him, said: "Shall I tell you what I think?"
41. The host assented. And Jesus said: "Well, it
is this. Two men held themselves debtors to a
certain man of property, one for five hundred
42. pence, the other for fifty. And neither the one
nor the other had anything to pay with. The
creditor pardoned both. Now, in your opinion,
which will love the creditor more, and show him
43. greater attention? And he said: "Of course,
44. he that owed more." Jesus pointed to the
woman, and said: "So it is with you and this
woman. You consider yourself orthodox, and
therefore a small debtor; she considers herself
an unbeliever, and therefore a great debtor. I
came to your house; you did not give me water
to wash my feet. She washed my feet with her
45. tears, and wiped them with her hair. You did
46. not kiss me, but she kissed my feet. You did
not give me oil to anoint my head, but she
47. anoints my feet with precious scent. He who
rests in orthodoxy will not do works of love, but
he who considers himself an unbeliever will do
works of love. And for works of love, all is
48-50. forgiven." And he said to her: "All your
wickedness is forgiven you." And Jesus said:
"All depends upon what each man considers
himself. Whoever considers himself good will
not be good; but whoever considers himself bad
will become good."
xviii. 10. And Jesus said further: "Two men once
came into a temple to pray; one orthodox, and

the other a tax-gatherer. The orthodox man Lk xviii. 11
prayed thus : 'I thank Thee, God, that I am not
as other men, I am not a miser, nor a libertine ;
I am not a rogue, not such a worthless fellow as
that tax-gatherer. I fast twice weekly, and give 12.
away a tithe of my property.' But the tax- 13.
gatherer stood afar off, and dared not look up
at the sky, but merely beat his breast, and said :
' Lord, look down upon me, worthless as I am.'
Well, and this man was better than the ortho- 14.
dox, for the reason that whoever exalts himself shall be humbled, and whoever humbles
himself shall be exalted."

After this, disciples of John came to Jesus, v. 33
and said : "Why do we and the orthodox fast
much, while your disciples do not fast ? For,
according to the law, God commanded people
to fast." And Jesus said to them : "While 34
the bridegroom is at the wedding, no one
grieves. Only when the bridegroom is away, 35.
do people grieve. Having life, one must not 36.
grieve. The external worship of God cannot
be combined with works of love. The old
teaching of the external worship of God cannot be combined with my teaching of works
of love to one's neighbor. To combine my
teaching with the old, is the same as to tear
off a shred from a new garment and sew it on
an old one. You will tear the new and not
mend the old. Either all my teaching must
be accepted, or all the old. And having once
accepted my teaching, it is impossible to keep
the old teaching, of purification, fasting, and
the Sabbath. Just as new wine cannot be 37.
poured into old skins, or the old skins will
burst and the wine run out. But new wine 38
must be poured into new skins, and both the
one and the other will remain whole."

CHAPTER III

THE SOURCE OF LIFE

The life of all men has proceeded from the spirit of the Father

("𝕳allowed be 𝕿hy Name")

M . xi. 2, 3.   AFTER this, John's disciples came to ask Jesus whether it was he of whom John spoke; whether he was revealing the kingdom of God,

4. and renewing men by the spirit? Jesus answered and said: " Look, listen, — and tell John, whether the kingdom of God has begun, and whether people are being renewed by the spirit. Tell him of what kingdom of God I

5. am preaching. It is said in the prophecies that, when the kingdom of God shall come, all men will be blessed. Well, tell him that

6. my kingdom of God is such that the poor are blessed, and that every one who understands me becomes blessed."

7. And, having dismissed John's disciples, Jesus began to speak to the people as to the kingdom of God John announced. He said: " When you went to John in the wilderness to be baptized, what did you go to see ? The orthodox teachers of the law also went, but did not understand that which John announced.

16. And they thought him nothing worth. This breed of orthodox teachers of the law only consider that as truth which they themselves invent and hear from each other, and that as law which they themselves have devised. But

18. that which John said, that which I say, they do not hearken to, and do not understand. Of that which John says, they have understood only that he fasts in the wild places, and

19. they say : ' In him is an evil spirit.' Of that which I say, they have understood only that

I do not fast, and they say: 'He eats and
drinks with tax-gatherers and sinners — he is
a friend of theirs.' They chatter with each   17
other like children in the street, and wonder
that no one listens to them. And their wis-   19.
dom is seen by their works. If you went to   8.
John to look at a man attired in rich clothes,
why, such dwell here in palaces. Then, what   9
did you go to seek in the desert? Did you go
because you think John was the same as other
prophets? Do not think this. John was not
a prophet like others. He was greater than
all prophets. They foretold that which might
be. He has announced to men that which
is, namely, that the kingdom of God was,
and is, on earth. Verily, I tell you, a man has   10.
not been born greater than John. He has
declared the kingdom of God on earth, and
therefore he is higher than all. The law and   Lk. xvi. 16.
the prophets, — all this was needful before
John. But, from John and to the present
time, it is announced that the kingdom of God
is on earth, and that he who makes an effort
enters into it."

And the orthodox came to Jesus, and began   xvii. 20.
asking him: "How, then, and when, will the
kingdom of God come?" And he answered
them: "The kingdom of God which I preach
is not such as former prophets preached.
They said that God would come with divers
visible signs, but I speak of a kingdom of
God, the coming of which may not be seen
with the eyes. And if any one shall say to
you, 'See, it is come, or it shall come,' or,
'See, it is here or there,' do not believe them.
The kingdom of God is not in time, or in
place, of any kind. It is like lightning, seen   24
here, there, and everywhere. And it has   21
neither time nor place, because the kingdom of
God, the one which I preach, is within you."

㎜ ⅲ. 1, After this, an orthodox believer, one of the
2. Jewish authorities, named Nicodemus, came
to Jesus at night, and said : " You do not bid
us keep the Sabbath, do not bid us observe
cleanliness, do not bid us make offerings, nor
fast ; you would destroy the temple.   You say
of God, He is a spirit, and you say of the kingdom of God, that it is within us. Then, what
kind of a kingdom of God is this ? "

3. And Jesus answered him : " Understand
that, if man is conceived from heaven, then
in him there must be that which is of heaven."

Nicodemus did not understand this, and
said : " How can a man, if he is conceived of
the flesh of his father, and has grown old,
again enter the womb of his mother and be
conceived anew ? "

5. And Jesus answered him : " Understand
what I say.   I say that man, besides the flesh,
is also conceived of the spirit, and therefore
every man is conceived of flesh and spirit, and
therefore may the kingdom of heaven be in
6. him.   From flesh comes flesh.   From flesh,
spirit cannot be born ; spirit can come only
8. from spirit.   The spirit is that which lives in
you, and lives in freedom and reason ; it is that
of which you know neither the beginning nor
the end, and which every man feels in him.
7. And, therefore, why do you wonder that I told
you we must be conceived from heaven ? "

9. Nicodemus said : " Still I do not believe that
this can be so."

10. Then Jesus said to him : "What kind of a
teacher are you, if you do not comprehend
11. this ?   Understand that I am not interpreting
some learned points ; I am interpreting that
which we all know, I am averring that which
12. we all see.   How will you believe in that
which is in heaven if you do not believe in that
which is on earth, which is in you yourself ?

"For, no man has ever gone up to heaven, but there is only man on earth, come down from heaven, and himself of heaven. Now, this same heavenly Son in man it is that must be lifted up, that every one may believe in him and not perish, but may have heavenly life. For God gave His Son, of the same essence as Himself, not for men's destruction, but for their happiness. He gave him in order that every one might believe in him, and might not perish, but have life without end. For He did not bring forth His Son, this life, into the world of men in order to destroy the world of men; but He brought forth His Son, this life, in order that the world of men might be made alive through him.

"Whoever commits his life to him does not die; but he who does not commit his life to him destroys himself thereby, in that he has not trusted to that which is life. Death consists in this, that life is come into the world, but men themselves go away from life.

"Light is the life of men; light came into the world, but men prefer the darkness to light, and do not go to the light. He who does wrong does not go to the light, so that his deeds may not be seen, and such a one bereaves himself of life. Whereas he who lives in truth goes to the light, so that his deeds are seen; and he has life, and is united with God.

"The kingdom of God must be understood, not, as you think, in the sense that it will come for all men at some time or other, and in some place or other, but thus, — In the whole world always, some people, those who trust in the heavenly Son of man, become sons of the kingdom, but others who do not trust in him are destroyed. The Father of that spirit which is in man is the Father of those only who acknowl-

Jn. iii. 13

14.

15.

16.

17.

18.

19.

20.

21.

edge themselves to be His sons. And, therefore, only those exist to Him who have kept in
themselves that which He gave them."

Mt xiii. 3. And, after this, Jesus began to explain to the
people what the kingdom of God is, and he
made this clear by means of parables.

He said: "The Father, — who is spirit, —
sows in the world the life of understanding,
4. as the husbandman sows seed in his field. He
sows over the whole field, without remarking
where any particular seed falls. Some seeds
fall upon the road, and the birds fly down and
5. peck them up. And others fall among stones;
and although among these stones they come
up, they wither, because there is no room for
7. the roots. And others, again, fall among wormwood, so that the wormwood chokes the corn,
8. and the ear springs up, but does not fill. And
others fall on good soil; they spring up, and
make return for the lost corn, and bear ears,
and fill, and one ear will give a hundredfold,
another sixtyfold, and another thirtyfold. Thus,
then, God also sowed broadcast the spirit in
men; in some it is lost, but in others it yields
a hundredfold: these last are they who form
Mk. iv. 26. the kingdom of God. Thus the kingdom is not
such as you think, that God will come to reign
over you. God has only sown the spirit, and
the kingdom of God will be in those who preserve it.

27. "God does not force men. It is as when the
sower casts the seeds in the earth, and himself
28. thinks no more of them; but the seeds of themselves swell, sprout up, put forth leaf, sheath,
29. and ear, and fill with grain. Only when it is
ripened, the master sends sickles to reap the
cornfield. So also God gave His Son, the
spirit, to the world; and the spirit of itself
grows in the world, and the sons of the spirit
make up the kingdom of God.

A woman puts yeast in the kneading trough Mt. xiii. 33
and mixes it with the flour; she then stirs it
no more, but lets it ferment and rise. As long
as men live, God does not interpose in their
life. He gave the spirit to the world, and the
spirit itself lives in men, and men who live by
the spirit make up the kingdom of God. For
the spirit there is neither death nor evil. Death
and evil are for the flesh, but not for the spirit.

The kingdom of God comes in this way.   24.
A farmer sowed good seed in his field. The
farmer is the Spirit, the Father; the field is
the world; the good seeds are the sons of the
kingdom of God. And the farmer lay down   25
to sleep, and an enemy came and sowed darnel
in the field. The enemy is temptation; the
darnel is the sons of temptation. And his   27.
laborers came to the farmer and said: "Can
you have sown bad seed?" Much darnel has
come up in your field. Send us, we will weed   28.
it out." And the farmer said: "You must   29.
not do that, for in weeding the darnel you will
trample the wheat. Let them grow together.
The harvest will come, when I shall bid the   30.
reapers take away the darnel and burn it; and
the wheat I shall store in the barn."

Now, the harvest is the end of man's life,
and the harvesters are the power of heaven.
And the darnel shall be burnt, but the wheat
shall be cleaned and gathered. Thus also, at
life's end, all shall vanish which was a guile of
time, and the true life in the spirit shall alone
be left. For the Spirit, the Father, there is no
evil. The spirit keeps that which it needs, and
that which is not of it does not exist for it.

The kingdom of God is like a net. The net   47.
will be spread in the sea, and will catch all
kinds of fish. And afterward, when it is   48.
drawn out, the worthless will be set aside and
thrown into the sea. So will it be at the end

of the age; the powers of heaven will take the good, and the evil will be cast away.

Mt. xiii. 10. And when he finished speaking, the disciples asked him how to understand these parables?

11. And he said to them: "These parables must be understood in two ways. I speak all these parables because there are some like you, my disciples, who understand wherein is the kingdom of God, who understand that the kingdom of God is within every man, who understand how to go into it; while others do not under-

14. stand this. Others look, but see not; they hearken, and do not understand, because their

15. heart has become gross. Therefore I speak these parables with two meanings, for both classes of hearers. To the others I speak of God, of what God's kingdom is to them, and they may understand this; while to you I speak of what the kingdom of God is for you — that kingdom which is within you.

18. "And see that you understand as you ought

19. the parable of the sower. For you the parable is this: Every one who has understood the meaning of the kingdom of God, but has not accepted it in his heart, to him temptation comes and robs him of that which has been

20. sown: this is the seed on the wayside. That which was sown on stones, is he who at once

21. accepts with joy. But there is no root in him, and he only accepts for a time; but let straits and persecution befall him, because of the meaning of the kingdom, and he straightway

22. denies it. That which was sown among the wormwood is he who understood the meaning of the kingdom, but worldly cares and the seductions of wealth strangle the meaning

23. in him, and he yields no fruit. But that which was sown on good soil is he who understood the meaning of the kingdom, and accepted it into his heart; such yield fruit, one a hundred-

fold, another sixtyfold, another thirtyfold. For Mt. xiii. 12
he who retains, to him much is given; while
from him who does not retain, the whole will
be taken.

"And, therefore, take care how you under- Lk. viii. 18.
stand these parables. Understand them so as
not to give way to deceit, wrong, and care;
but so as to yield thirtyfold, or sixtyfold, or a
hundredfold.

"The kingdom of heaven grows and spreads Mt. xiii. 31.
in the soul out of nothing, providing everything. It is like a birch seed, the very smallest of seeds, which, when it grows up, becomes
greater than all other trees, and the birds of
heaven build their nests in it."

CHAPTER IV

GOD'S KINGDOM

*Therefore the will of the Father is the life and welfare of
all men*

("Thy kingdom come")

AND Jesus went among the towns and vil- Mt. ix. 35.
lages, and taught all men the happiness of fulfilling the Father's will. Jesus was sorry for 36.
men, that they perish without knowing wherein
is the true life, and are driven about and suffer,
without knowing why, like sheep left without
a shepherd.

Once a crowd of people gathered to Jesus, v. 1.
to hear his teaching; and he went up on a hill
and sat down. His disciples surrounded him.

And Jesus began to teach the people as to 2.
what is the Father's will. He said : —

Blessed are the poor and homeless, for they Lk. vi. 20, 21.
are in the will of the Father. Even if they
hunger for a time, they shall be satisfied; and

if they grieve and weep, they shall be com-
forted.   If people look down upon them, and
thrust them aside and everywhere drive them
23. away, let them be glad at this; for the people
of God have ever been persecuted thus, and
they receive a heavenly reward.

24.   But woe to the rich, for they have already
got everything they wish, and will get nothing more.   They are now satisfied; but they
25, shall be hungry.   Now they are merry; but
26. they shall be sad.   If all praise them, woe to
them, because only deceivers get everybody's
praise.

Blessed are the poor and homeless, but
blessed only then, when they are poor, not
merely externally, but in spirit; as salt is good
only when it is true salt; not externally only,
but when it has the savor of salt.

So, you also, the poor and homeless, are the
teachers of the world; you are blessed, if you
know that true happiness is in being homeless
and poor.   But if you are poor only externally,
then you, like salt without savor, are good for
14. nothing.   You must be a light to the world;
therefore do not hide your light, but show it to
15. men.   For when one lights a candle, one does
not put it under a bench, but upon the table,
16. that it may light all in the room.   So, you also,
do not hide your light, but show it by your
works, so that men may see that you know the
truth, and, looking at your good works, may
understand your Heavenly Father.

17.   And do not think that I free you from the law.
I teach not release from the law, but I teach
18. the fulfilment of the eternal law.   As long as
there are men under heaven, there is an everlasting law.   There will be no law, only when
men shall of themselves act wholly according
to the eternal law.   And now I am giving you
19. the commandments of the eternal law.   And

if any one shall release himself, if only from one
of these short commandments, and shall teach
others that they may so release themselves, he
shall be least in the kingdom of heaven; while
he who shall fulfil them, and shall thereby teach
others, shall be the greatest in the kingdom of
heaven.   Because if your virtue be not greater   Mt.   1 2t
than the virtue of the orthodox leaders, you
will in no way be in the kingdom of heaven.

These are the commandments :—

I

In the former law it was said: "Do not   21.
kill." But if any one shall kill another, he
must be judged.

But I tell you, that every one is worthy of   22.
judgment who gets angry with his brother.
And still more to blame is he who abuses his
brother.

So that, if you wish to pray to God, re-   23.
member, first, whether there is no man who
may have something against you. If you remember that but one man considers you have
offended him, leave your prayer, and go first   24
and make peace with your brother; and then
you may pray.   Know that God wants neither
sacrifice nor prayer, but peace, concord, and
love among you.   And you may neither pray,
nor think of God, if there is but one man to
whom you do not bear love.

And so this is the first commandment: Do
not be angry, do not abuse; but having
quarreled, make peace in such a way that
no one may have cause for offense against
you.

II

Mt v. 31.   In the former law it was said : "Do not commit adultery ; and if you wish to put away your wife, give her a bill of divorce."

28.   But I tell you, if you are drawn by the beauty of a woman, you are already commit-
29. ting adultery. All sensuality destroys the soul, and therefore it is better for you to renounce the pleasure of the flesh than to destroy your life.

32.   And if you put away your wife, then, be-sides being vicious yourself, you drive her also into vice, and him who shall have to do with her.

And therefore, this is the second command-ment : Do not think that love toward woman is good ; do not admire the beauty of women, but live with the one to whom you have be-come united, and do not leave her.

III

33.   In the former law it was said : "Do not utter the name of the Lord your God in vain, do not call upon your God when lying, and do not dishonor the name of your God. Do not swear by Me in untruth, so as to profane your
34. God." But I tell you that every oath is a profanation of God.

35.   Therefore, swear not at all. Man cannot promise anything, because he is wholly in the
36. power of the Father. A man cannot turn one hair from gray to black ; how then shall he swear beforehand, that he will do this and that, and swear by God ? Every oath is a profanation of God, for, if a man shall have to fulfil an oath which is against the will of God, it must follow that he has sworn to go against

God's will; so that every oath is evil. But Mt. v 37
when men question you about anything, say:
"Yes," if yes, — "No," if no. Everything
added to this is evil.

Therefore, the third commandment is:
Swear nothing, to any one; say "Yes," when
it is yes, — "No," when it is no; and understand that every oath is evil.

IV

In the former law it was said: " He who de-   38.
stroys life, shall give a life for a life; an eye
for an eye, a tooth for a tooth, a hand for a
hand, an ox for an ox, a slave for a slave,"
and so on.

But I tell you: Do not wrestle with evil by   39.
evil. Not only do not take by law an ox for
an ox, a slave for a slave, a life for a life, but
do not resist evil at all. If any one wishes to   40.
take an ox from you by law, give him another;
if any one wishes to get your coat by law, give
him your shirt also; if any one strikes out your
tooth on one side, turn to him the other side.
If you are made to do one piece of work, do   41.
two. If men wish to take your property,   vi. 30.
give it to them. If they do not return your
money, do not ask for it.

And therefore: Do not judge, do not go to   37.
law, do not punish, and you yourself shall not
be judged, nor punished. Forgive all, and you
shall be forgiven, because if you shall judge
people, they will judge you also.

You cannot judge, because you, all men, are Mt. vii. 1.
blind, and do not see the truth. How, with   3.
obstructed eyes, will you discern the mote in
your brother's eye? You must first clear your
own eye. But whose eyes are clear? Can a Lk. vi 39
blind man lead a blind man? Both will fall

into the pit. Thus, also, they who judge and punish, like the blind, are leading the blind.

Lk. vi. 40. They who judge and condemn people to violent treatment, wounds, maiming, death, wish to teach people. But what else can come from their teaching, than that the pupil will learn his lesson, and will become quite like the teacher? What, then, will he do, when he has learnt his lesson? The same that the teacher does: violence, murder.

Mt. vii. 6. And do not think to find justice in the courts. To seek legal justice, to hand matters over to human courts, is the same as to cast precious pearls before swine; they will trample upon it, and tear you to pieces.

And, therefore, the fourth commandment is: However men may wrong you, do not resist evil, do not judge and do not go to law, do not complain and do not punish.

V

v. 43. In the former law it was said: "Do good to men of your own nation, and do evil to strangers."

44. But I tell you, love not only your own countrymen, but people of other nations. Let strangers hate you, let them fall upon you, wrong you; but you speak well of them, and

46. do them good. If you are only attached to your countrymen, why, all men are thus attached to their own countrymen, and hence

45. wars arise. Behave equally well toward men of all nations, and you will be the sons of the Father. All men are His children, and therefore all are brothers to you.

And, therefore, this is the fifth commandment: Behave equally well toward foreigners, as I told you to behave among yourselves.

Before the Father of all men there are neither different nations nor different kingdoms: all are brothers, all sons of one Father. Make no distinction among people as to nations and kingdoms.

And so: I. Do not be angry, but be at peace with all men. II. Do not seek delight in sexual gratification. III. Do not swear anything to any one. IV. Do not oppose evil, do not judge, and do not go to law. V. Do not make any distinction among men as to nationality, and love strangers like your own people.

All these commandments are contained in Mt vii. 12 this one: All that you wish people should do for you, do you even so to them.

Fulfil my teaching, not for men's praise. If vi 1. you do it for men, then from men you have your reward. But if not for men, then your reward is from the Heavenly Father. So that, 2. if you do good to men, do not boast about it before men. Thus hypocrites do, that men may speak well of them. And they get what they wish. But if you do good to men, do it 3. so that no one may see it, so that your left hand may not know what your right hand is doing. And your Father will see this, and will give 4. you what you need.

And, if you wish to pray, do not pray like 5. the hypocrites. Hypocrites love to pray in churches, in the sight of men. They do this for men's sake, and get in return from men that which they wish.

But, if you wish to pray, go where no one 6. may see you, and pray to your Father, the Spirit, and the Father will see what is in your soul, and will give you that which you wish in the spirit.

When you pray, do not chatter with your 7. tongue like the hypocrites. Your Father 8.

knows what you want before you open your lips.

Pray only thus :

Mt. vi. 9. *Our Father, without beginning and without end, like heaven !*

10. *May Thy being only be holy.*

May power be only Thine, so that Thy will be done, without beginning and without end, on earth.

11. *Give me food of life in the present.*

12. *Smooth out my former mistakes, and wipe them away ; even as I so do with all the mistakes*

13. *of my brothers, that I may not fall into temptation, and may be saved from evil.*

Because Thine is the power and might, and Thine the judgment.

Mk. xi. 25. If you pray, above all, bear no one any

26. malice. For if you do not forgive men their wrong-doing, the Father also will not forgive you yours.

Mt. vi. 16. If you fast, and go hungry, do not show it to men ; thus do the hypocrites, that people may see, and speak well of them. And people speak well of them, and they get what they

17, wish. But do not you do so ; if you suffer

18. want, go about with a cheerful face, that people may not see. But your Father will see, and will give you what you need.

19. Do not lay up store on earth. On earth, the worm consumes, and rust eats, and thieves

20. steal. But lay up heavenly wealth for yourself. Heavenly wealth the worm does not gnaw, nor

21. rust eat, nor thieves steal. Where your wealth is, there will your heart also be.

22. The light of the body is the eye, and the

23. light of the soul is the heart. If your eye is dim, then all your body will be in darkness. And if the light of your heart is dim,

then all your soul will be in darkness. You Mt. vi. 24
cannot serve at one time two masters. You
will please one, and offend the other. You cannot serve God and the flesh. You will either
work for the earthly life or for God. There- 25.
fore, do not be anxious for what you shall eat
and drink, and wherewith you shall be clothed.
Life is more wonderful than food and clothing,
and God gave it you.

Look at God's creatures, the birds. They do 26.
not sow, reap, or harvest, but God feeds them.
In God's sight, man is not worse than the bird.
If God gave man life, He will be able to feed
him too. But you yourselves know that, how- 27.
ever much you strive, you can do nothing for
yourselves. You cannot lengthen your life by
an hour. And why should you care about 28.
clothing? The flowers of the field do not 29.
work and do not spin, but are dressed as Solo-
mon in all his glory never was. Well, then, if 30.
God has so adorned the grass, which to-day
grows and to-morrow is mown, will he not
clothe you?

Do not trouble and worry yourselves; do 31.
not say that you must think of what you will
eat and how you will be clothed. This every 32.
one needs, and God knows this need of yours.
And so, do not care about the future. Live 33.
in the present day. Take care to be in the
will of the Father. Wish for that which alone
is important, and the rest will all come of itself.
Strive only to be in the will of the Father. 34.
And so, do not trouble about the future.
When the future comes, then it will be time to
do so. There is enough evil in the present.

Ask and it shall be given you, seek and you Lk. xi. 9.
shall find, knock and it shall be opened to you.
Is there a father who would give his son a Mt. vii. 9, 10.
stone instead of bread, or a snake instead of a
fish? Then, how is it that we, wicked men, 11.

are able to give our children that which they need, while your Father in heaven shall not give you that which you truly need, if you ask Him? Ask, and the Heavenly Father will give the life of the spirit to them who ask Him.

Mt. vii. 13. The way to life is narrow, but enter by the narrow way. The way into life is one only. It is narrow and strait. About it the plain lies great and wide, but it is the way of de-

14. struction. The narrow way alone leads to

Lk. xii. 32. life ; and few find it. But do not quail, little flock ! The Father has promised you the kingdom.

Mt. vii. 15. Only, beware of false prophets and teachers ; they approach you in sheepskins, but within they are ravening wolves.

16. By their fruits will you know them ; by that which they yield. Figs are not gathered from

17. thistles, nor grapes from thorns. But a good tree brings forth good fruit. And a bad tree

20. brings forth bad fruit. And so you will know

Lk. vi. 45. them by the fruits of their teaching. A good man, from his good heart, brings forth everything that is good ; but a wicked man, from his evil heart, brings forth everything evil ; for the lips speak from the overflow of the heart. And therefore, if teachers teach you to do to others that which is bad for yourselves, — teach violence, executions, wars, — know that they are false teachers.

Mt. vii. 21. For it is not he that says : Lord, Lord ! who shall enter the kingdom of heaven, but he who fulfils the word of the Heavenly Father.

22. The false teachers will say : " Lord, Lord ! we have taught your teaching, and we have driven

23. away evil according to your teaching." But I will disown them, and say to them : No, I never acknowledged you, and do not acknowledge you. Go out of my sight, you are doing that which is unlawful.

And so, every one who has heard these words Mt. vii. 24
of mine, and fulfils them, he, like a reasonable
man, builds his house upon a rock. And his   25.
house will stand against all storms. But he   26.
who hears these words of mine, and does not
fulfil them, he, like a foolish man, builds his
house upon sand. When the storm comes,   27.
it will overthrow the house, and all will perish.

And all the people wondered at such teaching; Lk. iv. 32.
because the teaching of Jesus was quite other
than that of the orthodox teachers of the law.
These taught a law which must be obeyed, but
Jesus taught that all men are free. And in Mt. iv. 14.
Jesus Christ were fulfilled the prophecies of
Isaiah : "The people living in darkness, in the   16.
shadow of death, saw the light of life, and he
who furnished this light of truth does no violence nor harm to men, but he is meek and
gentle. He, in order to bring truth into the   xii. 19.
world, neither disputes nor shouts ; his voice
is never heard raised. He will not break a   20.
straw, and will not blow out the smallest light.
And all the hope of men is in his teaching.   21.

CHAPTER V

THE TRUE LIFE

*The fulfilment of the personal will leads to death ; the fulfil-
ment of the Father's will gives true life*

("Thy will be done")

AND Jesus rejoiced at the strength of the Mt. xi. 25
spirit, and said : —
"I acknowledge the spirit of the Father, the
source of everything in heaven and earth, Who
has revealed that which was hidden from the
wise and learned, to the simple, solely through

their acknowledging themselves Sons of the Father.

Mt. xi. 28. "All take care for fleshly happiness, and have put themselves to a load which they cannot draw; they have put a yoke upon themselves which was not made for them.

"Understand my teaching and follow it; and you shall know rest and joy in life. I give you another yoke, and another load; 29. namely, the spiritual life. Put yourselves to that, and you shall learn from me peace and happiness. Be calm and meek in heart, and 30. you will find blessedness in your life. Because my teaching is a yoke made for you, and the fulfilment of my teaching is a light load, with a yoke made for you."

Jn. iv. 31. The disciples of Jesus once asked him 32. whether he wished to eat. He said: "I 33. have food of which you do not know." They thought that some one had brought him some- 34. thing to eat. But he said : —

"My food is to do the will of Him who gave me life, and to fulfil that which He intrusted 35, to me. Do not say 'There is still time,' as the 36. plowman said, waiting for the harvest. He who fulfils the will of the Father is always satisfied, and knows neither hunger nor thirst. The fulfilment of the will of God always satisfies, bearing its reward within itself. You must not say, 'I will afterward fulfil the will of the Father.' While there is life, you always can, and must, fulfil the will of the Father. 37. Our life is the field which God has sown, and 38. our business is to gather its fruits. And if we gather the fruits, we get the reward, life beyond time. True it is, that we do not give ourselves life; some one else does. And if we labor to gather in life, then we, like reapers, get our reward. I teach you to gather in this life, which the Father has given you."

Once, Jesus came to Jerusalem. And there ^{Jn.} ^{v. 1,} was then a bathing-place there. And men said ^{2,} ^{4.} of this bathing-place, that an angel came down into it, and through this the water in the bath would begin to move, and he who first plunged into the water after it was moved got well from whatever he was ailing. And sheds were made around the bath, and under these sheds sick men lay, waiting for the water in the bath to be moved, in order to plunge into it.

And a man was there who had been infirm thirty-eight years. Jesus asked who he was.

And the man told how he had been ailing so long, and was still waiting to get into the bath first, upon the water being moved, in order to be healed; but for these thirty-eight years he had been unable to get in first, others always getting into the bath before him.

And Jesus saw that he was old, and said to him: "Do you wish to get well?"

He said: "I wish to, but I have no one to carry me into the water in time. Some one always will get in before me."

And Jesus said to him: "Awake, take up your bed and walk."

And the sick man took up his bed and walked.

And it was the Sabbath. And the orthodox said: "You must not take up the bed, for to-day is the Sabbath." He said: "He who raised me, bade me also take up the bed." And the infirm man said to the orthodox, that it was Jesus who had healed him. And they became angry, and accused Jesus, because he did such things on the Sabbath.

And Jesus said: "That which the Father always does, I also do. In truth, I say to you, the Son of himself can do nothing. He does only that which he has understood from the Father. What the Father does, he also does.

The Father loves the Son, and by this very
fact has taught him everything which the Son
should know.

"The Father gives life to the dead, and
thus the Son gives life to him who desires it;
because, as the business of the Father is life,
22. so the business of the Son must be life. The
Father has not condemned men to death, but
has given men power, at will, to die or live.
23. And they will live, if they shall honor the
Son as the Father.

24.   "I tell you truly, that he who has understood the meaning of my teaching, and has
believed in the common Father of all men,
already has life, and is delivered from death.
25. They who have understood the meaning of
human life, have already escaped from death
26. and shall live forever. Because, as the
Father lives of Himself, so also has He given
27. the Son life within himself. And He has
given him freedom. It is by this, that he is
the Son of Man.

28.   "Henceforth all mortals shall be divided
29. into two kinds. They alone, who do good,
shall find life; but they who do evil shall be
30. destroyed. And this is not my decision, but
it is what I have understood from the Father.
And my decision is true, because I thus decide, not in order to do that which I wish, but
in order that all may do that which the Father
of all wishes.

31.   "If I were to assure all that my teaching is
true, this would not establish my teaching.
36. But there is that which establishes my teaching; namely, the conduct which I teach. That
shows that I do not teach of myself, but in the
37. name of the Father of all men. And my
Father, He who has taught me, confirms the
truth of my commandments in the souls of
all.

"But you do not wish to understand and to know His voice. And you do not accept the Jn.   v. 38 meaning this voice speaks. That that which is in you, is spirit descended from heaven, — this, you do not believe.

"Enter into the meaning of your writings. 39. You will find in them the same as in my teaching, commandments to live, not for yourself alone, but for the good of men. Why, then, do 40. you not wish to believe in my commandments, which are those that give life to all men? I 43. teach you in the name of the common Father of all men, and you do not accept my teaching; but if any one shall teach you in his own name, him will you believe.

"One cannot believe that which people say 44. to each other, but one can only believe that in every man there is a Son like the Father."

And that men may not think that the king- Lk. xix. 11. dom of heaven is established by anything visible; but that they may understand that the kingdom of God consists in the fulfilment of the Father's will; and understand that the fulfilment of the Father's will depends on each man's effort and striving to make people see that life is given, not for oneself personally, but for the fulfilment of the Father's will, which alone saves from death and gives life, — Jesus told a parable. He said : — 12.

"There was a rich man, who had to go away from his home. Before he went, he 13. called his slaves, and gave among them ten talents, one to each, and said : 'While I am away, labor each of you upon what I have given.' But it happened that, when he was gone, cer- 14. tain inhabitants of that town said : 'We do not 15. wish to serve him any more.' When the rich man came back, he called the slaves to whom he had given the money, and bade each say what he had done with his money. The first 16.

came, and said: 'See, master, for your one I
Lk. xix. 17. have earned ten.' And the master said to
him: 'Well done, good servant; you have
been trustworthy in a little, I will place you
over much; be one with me in all my wealth.'
18. Another slave came, and said: 'See, master,
19. for your talent I have earned five.' And the
master said to him: 'Well done, good slave,
20. be one with me in all my estate.' And yet
another came, and said: 'Here is your talent,
I hid it in a cloth and buried it; because I was
21. afraid of you. You are a hard man, you take
where you did not store, and gather where
22. you did not sow.' And the master said to
him: 'Foolish slave! I will judge you by your
own words. You say that, from fear of me,
you hid your talent in the earth, and did not
work upon it. If you knew that I was severe,
and take where I did not give, then why did
Mt. xxv. 26, you not do that which I bade you do? If you
Lk. xix. 23. had worked upon my talent, the estate would
have been added to, and you would have fulfilled that which I bade you. But you have
not done that for which the talent was given
you, and, therefore, you must not own it.'
24. And the master bade the talent be taken from
him who had not worked upon it, and given to
25. him who had worked most. And then the
servants said to him: 'Sir, he already has
26. much.' But the master said: 'Give to them
who have worked much, because he who looks
after that which he has, shall receive an in-
Mt. xxv. 30. crease. As to them who did not wish to be in
my power, drive them forth, so that they may
be here no more.'"

Now this master is the source of life, the
spirit, the Father. His slaves are men. The
talents are the life of the spirit. As the master does not himself work upon his estate, but
bids the slaves to work, each by himself, so

the spirit of life in men has given them the command to work for the life of men, and then left them alone. They who sent to say that they did not acknowledge the authority of the master, are they who do not acknowledge the spirit of life. The return of the master, and the demand for an account, is the destruction of fleshly life, and the decision of the fate of men as to whether they have yet life beyond that which was given them. Some, the slaves who fulfil the will of the master, work upon that which was given them, and make gain on gain; they are those men who, having received life, understand that life is the will of the Father, and is given to serve the life of others. The foolish and wicked slave, who hid his talent and did not work upon it, represents those men who fulfil only their own will, and not the will of the Father; who do not serve the life of others. The slaves who have fulfilled the master's will, and worked for the increase of his estate, become sharers of the whole estate of the master, while the slaves who have not fulfilled the master's will, and have not worked for him, are bereft of that which was given them. People who have fulfilled the will of the Father, and have-served life, becomes sharers in the life of the Father, and receive life, notwithstanding the destruction of the fleshly life. They who have not fulfilled the will, and have not served life, are bereft of that life which they had, and are destroyed. They who did not wish to acknowledge the authority of the master, such do not exist for the master; he drives them forth. People who do not acknowledge within themselves the life of the spirit, the life of the Son of man, such do not exist for the Father.

After this, Jesus went into a desert place. Jn. vi. 1, And many people followed him. And he 2. 3.

climbed a mountain, and sat there with his
followers.   And he saw that there was a great
throng, and said : " Whence shall we get bread
to feed all these people ? " Philip said : " Even
two hundred pence will not suffice, if to each
be given but a little.   We have only a little
bread and fish."   And another disciple said :
" They have bread ; I have seen it.   There is
a boy who has five loaves and two small fishes."

10.   And Jesus said : " Bid them all lie down on
the grass."

11.   And Jesus took the loaves which he had,
and gave them to his disciples, and bade them
give them to others ; and so all began to hand
from one to another what there was, and all
were satisfied, yet much was left over.

26.   The next day, the people came again to
Jesus.   And he said to them : " See, you come
to me, not because you have seen wonders,
but because you have eaten bread and were
27. satisfied."   And he said to them : " Work not
for perishable food, but for everlasting food,
such as only the spirit of the Son of Man gives,
sealed by God."

28.   The Jews said : " But what must we do, in
order to do the works of God ? "

29.   And Jesus said : " The work of God is in
this, to believe in that life which He has given
you."

30.   They said : " Give us a sign that we may
believe.   What are your deeds which can serve
31. as a proof ?   Our fathers ate manna in the wilderness.   God gave them bread from heaven
to eat ; and so it is written."

32.   Jesus answered them: " The true heavenly
bread is the spirit of the Son of Man, that
33. which the Father gives.   Because the nourishment of man is the spirit descended from
heaven.   This it is which gives life to the
35. world.   My teaching gives true nourishment

Jn.   vi. 5.

7.

Mt. xiv. 17.
Jn.   vi. 9.

to man. He who follows me shall not hunger, and he who believes in my teaching will
never know thirst.

"But I have already told you that you have Jn. vi. 36
seen this, yet do not believe.

"All that life which the Father gave the Son 37.
will be realized through my teaching; and every one who believes will be a sharer in it. I 38.
came down from heaven, not to do that which
I wish, but to do the will of the Father, of Him
who gave me life. But the will of the Father 39.
who sent me is this, that I should keep all that
life which He gave, and should not destroy anything of it. And therefore, herein is the will of 40.
the Father who sent me, that every one who
sees the Son, and believes in him, should have
everlasting life. And my teaching gives life
at the last day of the body."

The Jews were shocked at his saying that his 41
teaching was come down from heaven. They 42.
said : "Why, this is Jesus, the son of Joseph;
we know his father and mother. How, then,
can he say that his teaching has descended from
heaven ? "

"Do not debate as to who I am, and whence 43.
I am come," said Jesus. "My teaching is true, 44.
not because I declare, like Moses, that God
spoke with me on Sinai; but it is true because
it is in you also. Every one who believes my
commandments, believes, not because it is I who
speak, but because our common Father draws
him to Himself; and my teaching will give
him life at the last day. And it is written in 45.
the prophets, that all shall be taught by God.
Every one who shall understand the Father,
and shall learn to understand His will, thereby
yields himself to my teaching.

"That any man has seen the Father, this has 46.
never been, except he who is from God; he has
seen, and sees, the Father.

Jn. vi. 47.   " He who believes in me (in my teaching) has everlasting life.

48,   " My teaching is the nourishment of life.
49.   Your fathers ate manna, food straight from
50.   heaven, and yet they died.   But the true nourishment of life, which descends from heaven, is such, that he who is fed with it will not die.

51.   My teaching is this nourishment of life descended from heaven.   He who is fed with it lives forever.   And this nourishment which I teach is my flesh, which I give for the life of all men."

52.   The Jews did not understand what he said, and began to dispute as to how it was possible to give one's flesh for the nourishment of men, and why.

53.   And Jesus said to them : " If you shall not give up your flesh for the life of the spirit,
54.   there will be no life in you.   He who does not give up his flesh for the life of the spirit, has
55.   not real life.   That in me which gives up the flesh for the spirit, that alone lives.

" And therefore, our flesh is the true food
56.   for the real life.   That only which in me consumes my body, that which gives up the fleshly
57.   life for the true life, that only is I.   It is in me, and I am in it.   And as I live in the flesh by the will of the Father, similarly, that which lives in me lives by my will."

60.   And some of his disciples, when they heard this, said : " These are hard words, and it is difficult to understand them."

61.   And Jesus said to them : " Your ideas are so confused, that my sayings as to what man was, is, and always will be, seem difficult to
63.   you.   Man is the spirit in the flesh, and the spirit alone gives life, but the flesh does not give life.   In the words which seem so difficult to you, I have really said nothing more than that the spirit is life."

Afterward, Jesus chose seventy men out of Lk.   x.   1
his near friends, and sent them into those places
where he himself wished to go.   He said to   2.
them :—

"Many people do not know the blessing of
real life. I am sorry for all; and wish to teach
all.   But as the master is not enough for the
reaping of his field, so also I shall not suffice.
Go you, then, through the various cities, and   3.
everywhere proclaim the fulfilment of the will
of the Father.

"Say, The will of the Father is in this : Not
to be angered, not to be sensual, not to swear,
not to resist evil, and not to make any distinction between people.   And accordingly, do ye
in everything fulfil these commandments.

"I send you like sheep among wolves. Be Mt.   x. 16.
wise as snakes, and pure as doves.

"Before everything, have nothing of your Lk.   x. 4.
own; take nothing with you, neither wallet, nor
bread, nor money; only clothes upon your body,
and shoes.   Further, make no distinction be-   5.
tween people ; do not choose your hosts, where
you shall put up.   But in whichever house you Mt.   x. 12.
shall come first, stay there.   When you come
into the house, greet the master.   If he welcome you, stay ; if not, go into another house.

"For that which you shall say, they will hate   22.
you, and fall upon, and persecute you.   And   23.
when they shall drive you out, go into another
village ; and if they all drive you out of that,
go yet into another.   They will persecute you
as wolves hunt sheep; but do not quail, suffer
to the last hour.   And they will take you into
the courts, and will try you, and will flog you,
and will take you before the authorities, that
you may justify yourselves before them.   And   19.
when you shall be taken into the courts, be
not afraid ; and do not bethink yourselves
what you shall say.   The spirit of the Father

will speak through you, what is needful to be
said.

Mt.   x. 23.   "You will not have passed through all the
towns, before people will have understood your
teachings, and will turn to it.

27.   "And so, be not afraid. That which is
hidden in the souls of men will come forth.

26. That which you shall say to two or three will

28. spread among thousands. But chiefly, be not
afraid of those who may kill your body. To
your souls, they can do nothing. And so, do
not fear them. But be afraid lest both your
bodies and souls be destroyed, by your abstain-
ing from the fulfilment of the will of the

29. Father. That is what you have to fear. Five
sparrows are sold for a farthing, but even they

30. shall not die without the Father's will. And
a hair shall not fall from the head without the

31. Father's will. So then, what need you be
afraid of, seeing you are in the Father's will?

34.   " Not all will believe in my teaching. And
they who will not believe, will hate it ; because
it bereaves them of that which they love, and

Lk. xii. 49. strife will come of it. My teaching, like fire,

51. will kindle the world. And from it strife must

52, arise in the world. Strife will arise in every

53. house. Father against son, mother against
daughter; and their kin will become haters
of them who understand my teaching, and

xiv. 26. they will be killed. Because, for him who
shall understand my teaching, neither his
father, nor his mother, nor wife, nor children,
nor all his property, will have any weight."

Mk. iii. 22.   Then the learned orthodox gathered at
Jerusalem, and went to Jesus. Jesus was in

20. a village, and a crowd of people thronged into
the place, and stood around.

Mt. xii. 24.   The orthodox began to speak to the people,
in order that they might not believe in the
teaching of Jesus. They said that Jesus was

possessed; that if they should live by his commandments, there would then be yet more evil among the people than now. They said, that he drove out evil with evil.

Jesus called them to him, and said: "You say that I drive out evil with evil. But no power destroys itself. If it destroys itself, then it would not be. You would drive out evil with threats, executions, murders; but evil, nevertheless, is not destroyed, precisely because evil cannot make head against itself. But I drive out evil by other means than you do; that is to say, not with evil. Mt. xii. 25 26. 27.

"I drive out evil by summoning people to fulfil the will of the Spirit, the Father, who gives life to all. Five commandments express the will of the Spirit which gives happiness and life. And these commandments destroy evil. By their doing so, you have a proof that they are true. 28. 29.

"If men were not sons of one spirit, it would not be possible to overcome evil; as it is not possible to go into the house of a strong man, and rob it. In order to rob the house of a strong man, it is necessary first to bind the strong man. And men are bound thus in the unity of the spirit of life.

"And therefore I tell you, that every mistake of men, and every wrong interpretation, shall escape punishment; but false representation about the Holy Spirit, which gives life to all, shall not be forgiven to men. Should any one say a word against man, that is not important; but should any one say a word against that which is holy in man, against the spirit, this cannot pass unpunished. Gird at me as much as you like, but do not call evil the commandments of life which I have disclosed to you. It cannot pass unpunished, if a man shall call that good which is evil. 31. 32.

Mt. xii. 30.   "It is necessary to be at one with the spirit of life. He who is not at one with it, is against it. It is necessary to serve the spirit of life and of good in all men, and not in oneself 33. alone. You must either hold that life and happiness is good for the whole world, then love life and happiness for all men, or else hold life and happiness an evil, and then not love life and happiness for yourself. You must either hold a tree good, and its fruit good or else hold a tree bad, and its fruit bad. Because a tree is valued by its fruit."

CHAPTER VI

THE FALSE LIFE

Therefore, in order to receive the true life, man must on earth resign the false life of the flesh, and live by the spirit

("On Earth, as in Heaven")

Lk. viii. 19.   AND there came once to Jesus his mother
Mt. xii. 46. and brothers, who could in no way get to see him, because there was a great crowd around 47. him. And a man saw them, and went up to Jesus, and said: "Your family, your mother and brothers, are standing without, and wish to see you."

Lk. viii. 21.   And Jesus said: "My mother and my brothers are they who have understood the will of the Father, and fulfil it."

xi. 27.   And a woman said: "Blessed is the womb that has brought you forth, and the breasts that you have sucked."

28.   Jesus said to this: "Blessed only are they who have understood the spirit of the Father, and keep it."

ix. 57.   And a man said to Jesus: "I will follow you whithersoever you may go."

And Jesus said to him, in answer: "You Lk. ix. 58
cannot follow me; I have neither house nor
place to live in. Wild beasts have their lairs
and burrows, but man is everywhere at home,
if he lives by the spirit."

And it happened once that Jesus was, with Mk. iv. 35.
his followers, sailing a boat. He said: "Let
us pass over to the other side." A storm arose 37.
upon the lake, and the boat began to fill, so
that it nearly sank. And Jesus lay in the 38.
stern, and slept. They woke him, and said:
"Teacher, is it really all the same to you that
we are perishing?" And, when the storm had 40.
fallen, he said: "Why are you so timid? You
do not believe in the life of the spirit."

Jesus said to a man: "Follow me." Lk. ix. 59.

And the man said: "I have an aged father,
let me first bury him, and then I will follow
you."

And Jesus said to him: "Let the dead bury 60.
the dead, but do you, if you wish to truly live,
fulfil the will of the Father, and make that will
known everywhere."

And again, another man said: "I wish to be 61.
your disciple, and will fulfil the will of the
Father, as you command, but let me first settle
my family."

And Jesus said to him: "If the plowman look 62.
behind, he cannot plow. However strong the
reasons you have to look behind, so long as you
look behind, you cannot plow. You must forget
everything except the furrow you are driving;
then only can you plow. If you consider as
to what will be the outcome for the life of the
body, then you have not understood the real
life, and cannot live by it."

After this, it happened once that Jesus went x. 38.
with his disciples into a village. And a woman
named Martha invited him into her house.
Martha had a sister named Mary, who sat at 39.

the feet of Jesus, and listened to his teaching.
Lk. x. 40. But Martha was busy getting ready the meal.

And Martha went up to Jesus, and said: "Do you not see that my sister has left me alone to serve? Tell her to help me in the work."

41. And Jesus said to her in answer: "Martha, Martha! you trouble and busy yourself with many things, but only one thing is needful.

42. And Mary has chosen that one thing which is needful, and which none shall take from her. For true life the food of the spirit alone is needful."

ix. 23. And Jesus said to all: "Whoever wishes to follow me, let him forsake his own will, and let him be ready for all hardships and sufferings of the flesh at every hour; then only can

24. he follow me. Because he who wishes to take heed for his fleshly life will destroy the true life. And he who fulfils the will of the Father, even if he destroy the fleshly life, shall save the true

25. life. For, what advantage is it to a man if he should gain the whole world, but destroy or harm his own life?"

xii. 15. And Jesus said: "Beware of wealth, because your life does not depend upon your having more than others.

16. "There was a rich man, who had a great harvest of corn. And he thought to himself:

17, 18. Let me rebuild my barns. I will erect larger

19. ones, and gather there all my wealth. And I will say to my soul: 'There, my soul, you have everything after your desire; rest, eat,

20. drink, and live for your pleasure.' But God said to him: 'Fool, this very night your soul shall be taken; and all that you have stored up shall go to others.'

21. "And thus it happens with every one who provides for the bodily life, and does not live in God."

xiii. 2. And Jesus said to them: "Now, you say

that Pilate killed the Galileans. But were these Galileans any worse than other people, that this happened to them? In no way. We Lk. xiii. 3 are all such, and we shall all perish likewise, unless we find salvation from death.

"Or of those eighteen men, whom the tower 4 crushed in falling, were they particularly worse than all the other dwellers in Jerusalem? In no wise. If we do not find salvation, sooner 5 or later we shall perish in the same way. If 6 we have not yet perished as they, we must think of our position, thus: —

"A man had an apple tree growing in his garden. The master came into the garden, and saw there was no fruit on the tree. And 7 the master said to his gardener: 'It is now three years since I have watched this apple tree, and it is still barren. It must be cut down, for as it is, it only spoils the place. And the gardener answered: 'Let us wait yet 8 a little, master; let me dig it round. I will dung it, and let us see what it will be next summer. Maybe it will yield fruit. But if it yields nothing by the summer, well then, we will cut it down.'

"Likewise we, as long as we live by the flesh, and yield no fruit to the life of the spirit, are barren apple trees. Only by the mercy of some power are we yet left for a summer. And if we do not yield fruit we shall also perish, even like him who built the barn, like the Galileans, like the eighteen men crushed by the tower, and like all who yield no fruit; perishing, dying forever, by death.

"In order to understand this, there is no Lk. xii. 54 need of special wisdom; each one sees this for himself. For not only in domestic affairs, but in that also which happens in the whole world, are we able to reason and to foresee. If the wind is in the west, we say there will be rain,

Lk. xii. 55. and so it happens. But if the wind is from the south, we say there will be fair weather,

56. and so it is. How, then, is it that we are able to foresee the weather, and yet we cannot foresee that we shall all die and perish, and that the only salvation for us is in the life of the spirit, in the fulfilment of its will?"

xiv. 25. And a great multitude went with Jesus, and he once more said to all:—

26. "He who wishes to be my disciple, let him count for nothing father and mother, and wife and children, and brothers and sisters, and all his goods, and let him at every hour be ready

27. for anything. And only he who does as I do, only he follows my teaching, and only he is saved from death.

28. "Because every one, before beginning anything, will reckon whether that which he does is profitable, and if it is profitable, will do it, but if unprofitable, will abandon it. Every one who builds a house will first sit down and reckon how much money is wanted, how much he has, and whether that will suffice to finish

29. it. He will do this, so that it may not happen that he should begin to build, and not finish, for people to laugh at him.

30. "Likewise also, he who wishes to live the fleshly life must first reckon whether he can finish that with which he is busy.

31. "Every king, if he wishes to make war, will first think whether he can go to war with ten

32. thousand against twenty thousand. If he concludes that he cannot, then he will send ambassadors, and make peace, and will not make war. So also, let every man, before giving himself over to the fleshly life, bethink him whether he can wage war against death, or whether death is stronger than he; and whether it is not then better for him to make peace beforehand.

"And so, each of you should first examine Lk. xiv. 33
what he considers his own family, money, or
estate. And, when he has reckoned what all
this avails him, and understands that it avails
him nothing, then only can he be my disciple."

And upon hearing this, a man said: "That 15.
is very well, if there be indeed a life of the
spirit. But what if one abandons all, and
there be no such life?"

To this Jesus said: "Not so; every one knows
the life of the spirit. You all know it; but you
do not do that which you know. Not because
you doubt, but because you are drawn away
from the true life by false cares, and excuse
yourselves from it.

"This is like your conduct, like your deeds: 16
A master got ready a dinner, and sent to invite guests, but the guests began to decline.
One said: 'I have bought land, and I must 18.
go and look after it.' Another said: 'I have 19.
bought oxen, and I must try them.' A third 20.
said: 'I have taken a wife, and am going to
celebrate the wedding.' And the messengers 21.
came and told the master that no one was
coming. The master then sent the messengers to invite the beggars. The beggars did 22.
not refuse, but came. And when they were
come, there was still room left. And the mas- 23.
ter sent to call in still more, and said: 'Go and
persuade all to come to my dinner, in order
that I may have more people.' And they who
had refused, from want of leisure, found no
place at the dinner.

"All know that the fulfilment of the will of
the Father gives life, but do not go because
the guile of wealth draws them away.

"He who resigns false temporary wealth for
the true life in the will of the Father, does as
did a certain clever steward. There was a man vi. 1.

who was steward to a rich master. This steward saw that, sooner or later, the master would
drive him away, and that he would remain
without food, and without shelter. And the
steward thought to himself : 'This is what I
will do : I will privately distribute the master's
goods to the laborers ; I will reduce their debts,
and then, if the master drives me out, the
laborers will remember my kindness, and will
not abandon me.' And so the steward did.
He called the laborers, his master's debtors,
and rewrote their documents. For him who
owed a hundred he wrote fifty ; for him who
owed sixty, he wrote twenty, and similarly for
the rest. And the master learned this, and
said to himself : 'Well, he has done wisely ;
otherwise he would have had to beg his bread.
To me he has caused a loss, but his own
reckoning was wise.'

"For, in the fleshly life, we all understand
wherein is the true reckoning, but in the life
of the spirit, we do not wish to understand.
Thus must we do with unjust, false wealth, —
give it up, in order to receive the life of the
spirit. And if we regret to give up such trifles
as wealth for the life of the spirit, then this
life will not be given us. If we do not give
up false wealth, then our own true life will not
be given us.

"It is impossible to serve two masters at
one time ; to serve God and Wealth, the will
of the Father, and one's own will. Either one
or the other."

And the orthodox heard this. But loving
wealth, they jeered at him.

And he said to them : "You think that,
because men honor you on account of wealth,
you are really honorable. It is not so. God
does not look at the exterior, but looks at the
heart. That which stands high among men, is

abomination in the eyes of God. Now the Lk. xvi. 16
kingdom of heaven is attainable on earth,
and great are they who enter it. But there
enter it, not the rich, but those who have nothing. And this has always been so, both according to your law, and according to Moses,
and according to the prophets also. Listen. 17
How does it stand with rich and poor in your
way of thinking?

"There was a rich man. He dressed well, 19
led an idle and amusing life every day. And 20.
there was a vagrant, Lazarus, covered with
sores. And Lazarus came to the yard of the 21.
rich man, and thought there would be leavings
from the rich man's table, but Lazarus did not
get even the leavings, the rich man's dogs ate
up everything, and even licked Lazarus' sores.
And both these died, Lazarus and the rich 22.
man. And in Hades, the rich man saw, far 23.
off, Abraham; and behold, Lazarus, the beggar, was sitting with him. And the rich man '4.
said: 'Father Abraham, see, Lazarus the beggar is sitting with you. He used to wallow
under my fence. I dare not trouble you, but
send Lazarus the beggar to me; let him but
wet his finger in water, to cool my throat, because I am burning in the fire.' But Abraham 25.
said: 'But why should I send Lazarus into
the fire to you? You, in that other world, had
what you wished, but Lazarus only saw grief;
so that he ought now to be happy. Yes, and 26.
though I should like to help you, I cannot,
because between us and you there is a great
pit, and it is impossible to cross it. We are
living, but you are dead.' Then the rich man 27.
said: 'Well, Father Abraham, send Lazarus
the beggar to my home. I have five brothers; 28.
I am sorry for them. Let him tell everything
to them, and show how harmful wealth is; so
that they may not fall into this torture.' But 29.

Abraham said : 'As it is, they know the harm. They were told of it by Moses, and by all the **Lk. xvi. 30.** prophets.' But the rich man said : 'Still, it would be better if some one should rise from the dead, and go to them ; they would the **31.** sooner bethink themselves.' But Abraham said : 'But if they do not listen to Moses and the prophets, then, even if a dead man came to life, they would not listen, even to him.' "

"That one should share all with one's brother, and do good to everybody ; this all men know. And the whole law of Moses, and all the prophets, said only this : 'You know this truth, but cannot do it, because you love wealth.' "

Mk. x. 17. And a rich official among the orthodox went up to Jesus, and said to him : "You are a good teacher, what shall I do to receive everlasting life ? "

18. Jesus said : "Why do you call me good? Only the Father is good. But, if you wish to have life, fulfil the commandments."

19. The official said : "There are many commandments ; which do you mean ? "

And Jesus said : "Do not kill, Do not commit adultery, Do not lie, Do not steal. Further, honor your Father, and fulfil His will ; and love your neighbor as yourself."

20. But the orthodox official said : "All these commandments I have fulfilled from my childhood ; but I ask, what else must one do, according to your teaching ? "

21. Jesus looked at him, at his rich dress, and smiled, and said : "One small thing you have left undone. You have not fulfilled that which you say. If you wish to fulfil these commandments : Do not kill, Do not commit adultery, Do not steal, Do not lie, and, above all, the commandment : Love your neighbour as yourself, — then, at once sell all your goods, and give them to the poor. Then you will have fulfilled the Father's will."

Having heard this, the official frowned, and Mk. x. 22 went away, because he was loath to part with his estates.

And Jesus said to his disciples: "As you 23. see, it is in no wise possible to be rich, and to fulfil the Father's will."

The disciples were horrified at these words, 24. so Jesus once more repeated them, and said: "Yes, children, he who has his own property, 25. cannot be in the will of the Father. Sooner Lk. xviii. 25. may a camel pass through a needle's eye than he who trusts in wealth fulfil the will of the Father." And they were still more horrified, 26. and said: "But, in that case, is it at all possible to keep one's life?"

He said: "To man it seems impossible to 27. support one's life without property; but God, even without property, can support a man's life."

Once, Jesus was going through the town of xix. 1. Jericho. And in this town was the chief of 2 the tax-gatherers, a rich man named Zaccheus. This Zaccheus had heard of the teaching of 3. Jesus, and believed in it. And when he knew that Jesus was in Jericho, he wished to see him. But there were so many people around, that it was impossible to push through to him. Zaccheus was short of stature. So he ran 4. ahead and climbed a tree, in order to see Jesus as he was going past. And thus, in passing 5. by, Jesus saw him, and having learnt that he believed his teaching, said: "Come down from the tree, and go home; I will come to your house." Zaccheus climbed down, ran home, 6. made ready to meet Jesus, and joyfully welcomed him.

The people began to criticize, and to say of 7.

Jesus: " See, he has gone into the tax-gatherer's house, — the house of a rogue."

Lk. xix. 8. Meanwhile, Zaccheus said to Jesus: " See, sir, this is what I will do. I will give away half of my goods to the poor, and out of what is left I will repay fourfold those whom I have wronged."

9. And Jesus said: " Now you have saved yourself. You were dead, and are alive; you were lost, and are found; because you have done as Abraham did, when he wished to slay his son;

10. you have shown your faith. Therein is the whole business of man's life; to seek out and save in his soul that which is perishing. But such sacrifice as yours must not be measured by its amount."

Mk. xii. 41. It happened once that Jesus and his disciples were sitting opposite a collecting-box. People were placing their contributions in the box, for God's service. Rich people went up to the box,

42. and put in much. And a poor woman, a widow, came and put in two farthings.

43. And Jesus pointed her out, and said: " See, now, this poor widow has put two farthings in

44. the box. She has put in more than all. Because they put in that which they did not need for their own livelihood; while this woman has put all that she had; she has put in her whole life."

Mt xxvi. 6. It happened that Jesus was in the house of

7. Simon the leper. And a woman came into the house. And the woman had a vase of precious oil worth fifteen pounds. Jesus said to his disciples, that his death was near. The woman heard this, and pitied Jesus, and, to show him her love, wished to anoint his head with the oil. And she forgot everything, and broke the vase, and anointed his head and feet, and poured out all the oil.

8. And the disciples began to discuss among

themselves, thinking that she had done wrong.
And Judas, he who afterward betrayed Jesus,
said: "See how much good stuff has gone for
nothing.   This oil might have been sold for fif- Mt. xxvi. 9
teen pounds, with which, how many poor might
have been helped!"   And the disciples began
blaming the woman; who was troubled, and did
not know whether she had done well or ill.

Then Jesus said: "You are troubling the   10.
woman without cause.   She has, indeed, done a
good work, and you mistakenly think of the poor.
If you wish to do good to the poor, do so; they   11.
are always with you.   But why call them to mind
now?   If you pity the poor, go with your pity,
do them good.   But she has pitied me, and done
real good, because she has given away all that
she had.   Who of you can know what is useful,
and what is not necessary?   How do you know
that there was no need to pour the oil over me?
She has thus anointed me with oil, and if it
were but to get ready my body for burial, this
was needful.   She truly fulfilled the will of the   13
Father, in forgetting herself and pitying another.
She forgot the reckonings of the flesh and gave
away all that she had."

And Jesus said: "My teaching is the fulfilment of the Father's will; and the Father's
will can be fulfilled by deeds only; not by
mere words.   If a man's son, in answer to his   xxi. 28
father's bidding, keeps saying, 'I obey, I
obey,' but does nothing which his father bids,
he then does not fulfil the will of his father.
But if another son keeps saying, ' I do not wish   29
to obey,' and then goes and does his father's
bidding, he indeed fulfils the father's will.
And so with men: Not he is in the Father's
will who says: 'I am in the Father's will,' —
but he who does that which the Father
wishes."

CHAPTER VII

I AND THE FATHER ARE ONE

The true food of everlasting life is the fulfilment of the Father's will

("𝕲𝖎𝖛𝖊 𝖚𝖘 𝖔𝖚𝖗 𝖉𝖆𝖎𝖑𝖞 𝖇𝖗𝖊𝖆𝖉")

Jn. vii. 1.   AFTER this the Jews tried to condemn Jesus to death, and Jesus went away into Galilee, and lived with his relations.

The Jewish feast of tabernacles was come.
2, And the brothers of Jesus got ready to go to
3. the feast, and invited him to go with them.
5. They did not believe in his teaching, and said
3. to him : —

"Now, you say that the Jewish service of God is wrong, that you know the real service of God by deeds. If you really think that no one but yourself knows the true service of God, then come with us to the feast. Many people will be there, and you can declare before them all that the teaching of Moses is wrong. If all believe you, then it will be clear to your disciples also, that you are right. Why
4. make a secret of it ? You say that our service is wrong, that you know the true service of God ; well then, show it to all."

6.   And Jesus said : " For you, there is a special time and place in which to serve God ; but for me, there is none. I always and everywhere
7. work for God. This is just what I show to people. I show to them that their service of God is wrong, and therefore do they hate me.
8. Go you to the feast, and I will go when I think fit."

9,   And the brothers went, but he remained
10. behind, and only came up at the middle of
11. the feast. And the Jews were shocked at

his not honoring their feast, and delaying to
come. And they discussed his teaching much. Jn vii. 12
Some said that he spoke the truth, while
others said that he only disturbed the people.

At the middle of the feast, Jesus entered 14.
the temple, and began to teach the people
that their service of God was wrong; that
God should be served not in the temple and
by sacrifices, but in the spirit, and by deeds.
All listened to him and wondered that he 15.
knew the whole of wisdom without having
learnt. And Jesus, having heard that all 16.
wondered at his wisdom, said to them : —

" My teaching is not my own, but His who
sent me. If any one wishes to fulfill the will 17.
of the Spirit which sent us into life, he will
know that I have not invented this teaching,
but that it is of God. Because he who invents 18.
from himself, follows his own mere imagina-
tions ; but he who seeks the mind of Him
who sent him, he is right, and there is no
wrong in him.

"Your law of Moses is not the Father's law, 19.
and, therefore, they who follow it do not fulfil
the Father's law, but work evil and falsehood.
I teach you the fulfilment of the will of the 21.
Father alone, and in my teaching there cannot 22.
be contradiction. But your written law of 23.
Moses is all full of contradictions. Do not 24.
judge by outside appearance, but judge by the
spirit."

And some said : " While he has been called 25.
a false prophet, see, he condemns the law, and
no one makes a charge against him. Maybe 26.
in very deed he is a true prophet ; maybe even
the authorities have acknowledged him. Only 27.
one reason makes it impossible to believe
him, namely, that it is said, when he who is
sent from God shall come, no one will know

whence he is come; but we know this man's birth and all his family."

The people still did not understand his teaching, and still sought proofs.

Jn. v i. 28.   Then Jesus said to them : "You know me, and whence I am, after the flesh. But you do not know whence I am, after the spirit. You do not know Him, from whom I am according to the spirit; and that is the only needful

19. knowledge. If I had said that I am Christ, you would have believed me, the Man, but you would not have believed the Father who is in me, and in you. But it is necessary to believe the Father only.

33. "I am here among you for the short space of my life. I point out to you the way to that source of life, from which I have come forth.

34. And you ask of me proofs, and wish to condemn me. If you do not know the way, then, when I shall be no more, you will in nowise find it. You must not discuss me, but must follow me. Whoever shall do that which I say, he shall know whether what I say is true. He for whom the fleshly life has not become the food of the spirit, he who follows not the truth, thirsting for it as for water, cannot

37. understand me. But he who thirsts for the

38. truth, let him come to me to drink. And he who shall believe in my teaching shall receive the

39. true life. He shall receive the life of the spirit."

40. And many believed in his teaching, and said : "That which he says is the truth and is of God."

42. Others did not understand him, and still sought in prophecies for proofs that he was sent from

43. God. And many disputed with him, but none

44. could controvert him. The learned orthodox

45. sent their assistants to contend with him, but their assistants returned to the orthodox priests and said : "We can do nothing with him."

And the high priests said to them : "But why

have you not convicted him?" And they an- Jn. vii. 46
swered: "Never did any man speak as he."

Then the orthodox said: "It signifies noth- 47.
ing that it is impossible to controvert him, and
that the people believe in his teaching. We do 48.
not believe, and none of the authorities believe.
But the people is cursed, they were always stu- 49.
pid and unlearned; they believe every one."

And Nicodemus, the man to whom Jesus ex- 50.
plained his teaching, said to the high priests:
"It is impossible to condemn a man without 51.
having heard him to the end, without understanding whither he is leading." But they said 52.
to him: "It is useless to discuss, or pay any attention to this affair. We know that a prophet
cannot come from Galilee."

At another time, Jesus was speaking with the viii. 12
orthodox, and said to them: "There can be no
proofs of the truth of my teaching, as there cannot be of the illumination of light. My teaching is the real light, by which people tell what
is good and what is bad, and therefore it is impossible to prove my teaching; which itself
proves everything. Whoever shall follow me
shall not be in darkness, but shall have life.
Life and enlightenment, which are one and the
same."

But the orthodox said: "You alone say this." 13.

And he answered them and said: "And if I 14.
alone say this, yet I am right; because I know
whence I came, and whither I go. According
to my teaching, there is reason in life; whereas,
according to yours, there is none. Besides this, 18.
not I alone teach, but my Father, the Spirit,
teaches the same."

They said: "Where is your Father?" 19.

He said: "You do not understand my teaching, and therefore you do not know my Father.
You do not know whence you are and whither 21
you go. I lead you, but you, instead of follow-

ing me, discuss who I am. Therefore you cannot come to that salvation of life to which I

Jn. viii. 24. lead you. And you will perish, if you remain
in this error, and do not follow me."

And the Jews asked : " Who are you ? "

26. He said : " From the very beginning, I tell
you, I am the Son of Man, acknowledging the

27. Spirit as my Father. That which I have understood of the Father, the same I tell to the

28. world. And when you shall exalt in yourselves the Son of Man, then you shall know
what I am ; because I do and speak, not of
myself, as a man, but I do and speak that
which the Father has taught me. This I say,
this I teach.

29. "And he who sent me is always with me ;
and the Father has not left me, because I do

31. His will. Whoever will keep to my understanding of life, whoever will fulfil the will of the
Father, he will be truly taught by me. In
order to know the truth, it is necessary to do
good to men. He who does evil to men, loves
darkness, and goes into it ; he who does good
to men, goes to the light ; so that, in order to
understand my teaching, it is necessary to do

32. good deeds. He who shall do good, shall know
the truth ; he shall be free from evil and death.

34. Because every one who errs becomes the slave
of his error.

35. "And as the slave does not always live in
the house of the master, while the son of the
master is always in the house, so also a man,
if he errs in his life and becomes a slave
through his errors, does not live always, but
dies. Only he who is in the truth remains
always living. The truth is in this, to be not
a slave, but a son. So that, if you err, you will

36. be slaves and die. But if you are in the truth,
then you shall be free sons, and shall be living.

37. "You say of yourselves that you are sons of

Abraham, that you know the truth. But see, you wish to kill me, because you do not understand my teaching. It comes to this, that I Jn. viii. 38 speak that which I have understood from my Father, and you wish to do that which you have understood from your father."

They said: "Our father is Abraham." 39

Jesus said to them : "If you were the sons of Abraham you would do his deeds. But see, 40. you wish to kill me because I told you that which I had learnt from God. Abraham did not do in that way ; therefore you do not serve God, but serve your father, another one."

They said to him : " We are not bastards, 41. but we are all children of our Father, all sons of God."

And Jesus said to them : "If your father 42. were one with me, you would love me, because I came forth from that Father. For I was not born of myself. You are not children of 43. the one Father with me, therefore you do not understand my word ; my understanding of life does not find place in you. If I am of the Father, and you of the same Father, then you cannot wish to kill me. But if you wish to kill me, then we are not of one Father.

"I am from the Father of good, from God ; 44. but you are from the devil, from the father of evil. You wish to do the lusts of your father the devil, who is always a murderer, and a liar, with no truth in him. If he, the devil, says anything, he says what is of himself, and not common to all, and he is the father of lying. Therefore you are the servants of the devil and his children. Now you see how plainly 46. you are convicted of error. If I err, then convict me ; but if there is no error in me, then why do you not believe in me ? "

And the Jews began to revile him, and to 48. say he was possessed.

Jn. viii 49.   He said : " I am not possessed ; but I honor
the Father, and you wish to kill me ; therefore
you are not brothers of mine, but children of
50. another father.   It is not I that affirm that I
51. am right, but the truth speaks for me.   Therefore I repeat to you : he who shall comprehend
my teaching and perform it, shall not see death."

52.   And the Jews said : " Well, do not we speak
the truth in saying that you are a Samaritan
possessed, and that you convict yourself ?   The
prophets died, Abraham died ; but you say that
he who performs your teaching shall not see
53. death.   Abraham died, and shall you not die ?
Or are you greater than Abraham ? "

54.   The Jews were still discussing as to whether
he, Jesus of Galilee, was an important prophet,
or unimportant, and forgot that he had told them
that he said nothing of himself as a man, but
spoke of the spirit that was within him.

And Jesus said : " I do not make myself to
be anything.   If I spoke of myself, of that
which only seems to me, then all that I should
say would mean nothing.   But there is that
source of everything which you call God ; well,
55. it is of Him that I speak.   But you have not
known, and do not know the true God.   But
I know Him, and I cannot say that I do not
know Him ; I should be a liar like you, if I
said that I do not know Him.   I know Him,
56. and know His will, and fulfil it.   Abraham,
your father, saw and rejoiced over my understanding."

57.   The Jews said : " You are only thirty years
old. how were you living at the same time as
Abraham ? "

58.   He said : " Before Abraham was, there was
the understanding of good, there was that which
I tell you."

59.   Then the Jews picked up stones in order to
kill him, but he went away from them.

Jesus said : " My teaching is the awakening Jn. xi. 25
of life. He who believes in my teaching, notwithstanding that he dies in the flesh, remains
living, and every one who lives and believes in 26.
me shall not die."

And yet a third time Jesus taught the peo- x. 1.
ple ; he said : " Men surrender themselves to
my teaching, not because I myself prove it.
It is impossible to prove the truth. The truth
itself proves all the rest. But men surrender
to my teaching, because there is no other than
it ; it is known to men, and promises life.

" My teaching is to men as the shepherd's 2,
3.
familiar voice is to the sheep, when he comes
among them through the door, and gathers
them, to lead them to the pasture. But your 5.
teaching, no one believes ; because it is foreign
to them, and because they see in it your own
lusts. It is with men as with sheep, at the
sight of a man who does not enter by the door,
but climbs over the fence. The sheep do not
know him, but feel that he is a robber. My 7.
teaching is the only true teaching ; like the one
door for the sheep. All your teachings of the 8.
law of Moses are lies, they are all like thieves
and robbers to the sheep. He who shall give 9.
himself up to my teaching shall find true life ;
just as the sheep go forth and find food, if they
follow the shepherd.

" A thief only comes to steal, rob, and de- 10.
stroy, but the shepherd comes to give life.
And my teaching alone promises, and gives
the true life.

" There are shepherds to whom the sheep 11.
are the chief interest in life, and who give up
their lives for the sheep. These are true 12
shepherds. And there are hirelings who do
not care about the sheep, because they are hirelings, and the sheep are not theirs ; so that if
a wolf comes they abandon their charge and

flee from them, and the wolf devours the sheep.

Jn. x. 13. These are false shepherds. And so there are false teachers, such as have no concern with the life of people; while true teachers give up their lives for the life of men.

14, 17. "I am such a teacher. My teaching is this,—to give up one's life for the life of men.

18. No one shall take my life from me, but I myself freely give it up for men, in order to receive true life. The commandment to do this I re-

15. ceived from my Father. And as my Father knows me, so I also know Him; and therefore

17. I lay down my life for men. Therefore the Father loves me, because I fulfil His commandments.

16. "And all men, not only those here now, but all men, shall understand my voice; and all shall come together into one, and all men shall be one, and their teaching one."

24. And the Jews surrounded him, and said: "All that you say is difficult to understand, and does not agree with our writings. Do not torment us, but simply and straightforwardly tell us, whether you are that Messiah who, according to our writings, should come into the world."

25. And Jesus answered them: "I have already told you who I am, but you do not believe. If you do not believe my word, then believe my works; by them understand who I am, and wherefore I am come.

26. "But you do not believe me because you do
27. not follow me. He who follows me, and does
28. that which I say, he understands me. And he who understands my teaching and fulfils it, re-
29. ceives the true life. My Father has united
30. them with me, and no one can disunite us. I and the Father are one."

31. And the Jews were offended at this, and took up stones to kill him.

But he said to them: "I have shown you   Jn. x. 32
many good works, and have disclosed the
teaching of my Father.   For which, then, of
these good works do you wish to stone me?"

They said: "Not for the good do we wish   33
to stone you; but because you, a man, make
yourself God."

And Jesus answered them: "Why, this is   34
just what is written in your writings, where
it says that God Himself said to the wicked
rulers: 'You are gods.'   If He called even   35.
vicious men gods, then why do you consider   36.
it sacrilege to call that the son of God, which
God in His love sent into the world?   Every
man in the spirit is the son of God.   If I do   37.
not live in God's way, then do not believe that
I am a son of God.   But if I live after God's   38.
way, then believe from my life that I am in
the Father, and then you will understand that
the Father is in me and I in Him."

And the Jews began to dispute.   Some said   20.
that he was possessed, and others said: "A   21.
man who is possessed cannot enlighten men."
And they did not know what to do with him,   39.
and could not condemn him.   And he went   40.
again across the Jordan, and remained there.
And many believed in his teaching, and said   41.
that it was true, as the teaching of John was.
Therefore many believed in it.   42.

And Jesus once said to his disciples: "Tell   Mt. xvi. 13.
me how the people understand my teaching
about the son of God and the son of man."

They said: "Some understand it like the   14.
teaching of John, others like the prophecies of
Isaiah; others, again, say that it is like the
teaching of Jeremiah.   They understand that
you are a prophet."

" And how do you understand my teaching?"   15.

And Simon Peter said to him: "In my   16.
opinion, your teaching consists in this, that

you are the chosen Son of the God of Life.
You teach that God is the life in man."

Mt. xvi. 17. And Jesus said to him: "Happy are you,
Simon, that you have understood this. No
man could disclose this to you; but you have
understood this, because God in you has disclosed it to you. Not fleshly understanding,
and not I, my words, have disclosed this to
you; but God my Father has directly disclosed

18. it. And upon this is founded that society of
men for whom there is no death."

CHAPTER VIII

LIFE IS NOT TEMPORAL

Therefore true life is to be lived in the present

("𝕿𝖍𝖎𝖘 𝖉𝖆𝖞")

Mt. x. 38. JESUS said: "He who is not ready for all
fleshly sufferings and bereavements, has not

39. understood me. He who shall obtain all that
is best for the fleshly life, shall destroy the true
life; he who shall destroy his fleshly life in fulfilling my teaching, shall receive the true life."

xix. 27. And in answer to these words, Peter said
to him: "See, we have listened to you, have
thrown off all cares and property, and have followed you. What reward shall we have for
this?"

Mk. x. 29, And Jesus said to him: "Every one who
30. has abandoned home, sisters, brothers, father,
mother, wife, children, and his fields, for my
teaching, shall receive a hundredfold more than
sisters and brothers and fields, and all that is
needful in this life; and besides this, he re-

31. ceives life beyond the power of time. There
are no rewards in the kingdom of heaven, the
kingdom of heaven is its own aim and reward.

In the kingdom of God all are equal, there is neither first nor last.

"Because the kingdom of heaven is like this. Mt xx. 1. The master of a house went in the early morning to hire laborers for his grounds. He 2. hired laborers at a penny a day, and set them to work in the garden. And he again went at 3. mid-day and hired more, and sent them into the garden to work; and at evening he hired still more, and sent them to work. And with them all he agreed at a penny. The time 8. came for the reckoning. And the master ordered all to be paid alike. First, those who 9. came last; and afterward, the first. And the first saw that the last received each a penny. And they thought that they would receive 10. more; but the first were also given each a penny. They took it and said: 'But how is 11. this? They only worked one shift, and we all 12. four; why, then, do we receive alike? This 13. is unjust.' But the master came up, and said: 'What are you complaining about? Have I offended you? The amount I hired you for, I have given you. Our agreement was for a 14. penny, take it and go. If I wish to give to the last the same as to you, am I not master of my own will? Or because you see that I 15. am good, is that the cause of your grudging?'"

In the kingdom of God there is neither first 16. nor last, for all there are as one.

There came to Jesus two of his disciples, 20. James and John, and said: "Promise us that Mk x. 35. you will do that for us which we shall ask of you."

He said: "What do you wish?" Mt. xx. 21.

They said: "That we may be equal with you."

Jesus said to them: "You yourselves do not 22 know what you ask. You may live just as I do, and be cleansed from fleshly life like me,

but to make you like myself is not in my
Mt. xx. 23. power. Every man may, by his own effort,
enter the kingdom of his Father, having sub-
mitted to His power, and fulfilling His will."

24. When they heard of this, the other disciples
grew angry with the two brothers, because
these wished to be equal to their teacher, and
the first among his disciples.

25. But Jesus called them, and said: "If you
brothers, James and John, asked me to make
you such as I am in order to be first among
my disciples, then you were mistaken; but if
you, my other disciples, are angry with them
because they wish to be your elders, then you
also are mistaken. Only in the world are
kings and officials reckoned by seniority for
governing the people. But among you, there
26. cannot be either elder or younger. Among
you, for one to be greater than another, it is
27. necessary to be the servant of all. Among
you, let him who wishes to be first, consider
28. himself last. Because therein is the will of
the Father as to the Son of Man; who does
not live to be served, but to himself serve all,
and to give up his fleshly life, as a ransom for
the life of the spirit."

xviii. 11. And Jesus said to the people: "The Father
12. seeks to save that which perishes. He rejoices over it, as a shepherd rejoices when he
has found one sheep that was lost. When
one is lost, he leaves the ninety-nine, and goes
Lk. xv. 8. to save the lost one. And if a woman lose a
farthing, she will sweep out the whole hut and
10. seek until she find it. The Father loves the
Son, and calls him to Himself."

xiv. 8. And he told them yet another parable, to
the effect that they who live in the will of
God ought not to exalt themselves. He said:
"If you are invited to dinner, do not seat
yourself in the front corner; some one will

come of more consideration than yourself, and
the master will say: 'Leave your place, and
allow him who is better than you to be seated.'
Then you will be put to shame. But do better,
take your seat in the very last place, then the
master will find you, and call you to a place
of honor, and you will be honored. Lk. xiv. 9. 10.

"So also in the kingdom of God there is no
room for pride. He who exalts himself, by so
doing lowers himself; but he who humbles
himself, and considers himself unworthy, by
this same means raises himself in the kingdom
of God. 11.

"A man had two sons. And the younger
said to his father: 'Father, give me my property.' And the father gave him his share.
The younger son took his share, went abroad,
squandered all his property, and began to
suffer want. And abroad, he became a swine-
herd. And he so hungered, that he ate acorns
with the swine. And he bethought himself of
his life, and said: 'Why did I take my share
and leave my father? My father had plenty
of everything; at my father's, even laborers
ate their fill. But I here am eating the same
food as the swine. I will go to my father, fall
at his feet, and say: I am to blame, father,
before you, and am not worthy to be your
son. Take me back even as a laborer.'
So he thought, and he went to his father.
And when he was still far off, his father at
once recognized him, and himself ran to meet
him, embraced him, and began to kiss him.
And the son said: 'Father, I am to blame
before you, I am not worthy to be your son.'
But the father would not even listen, and said
to the laborers: 'Bring quickly the best
clothes and the best boots, to clothe him and
shoe him. And go and bring a fatted calf and
kill it, and we will rejoice that this my son was xv. 11. 12. 13. 15. 16. 17. 18. 20. 21. 22. 23. 24.

dead and is now alive, was lost and is now
Lk xv. 25. found.' And the elder brother came from
the field, and as he approached he heard the
26. sounds of music in the house. He called a
servant to him, and said: 'Why is there this
merry-making here?' And the boy said:
27. 'Have you not heard that your brother is
returned, and your father is full of joy, and
has ordered a fatted calf to be killed, for joy
28. that his son has returned?' The elder brother
was offended, and did not go into the house.
29. And the father came out and called him. And
he said to his father: 'See, father, how many
years I have worked for you, and have not
disobeyed your command, while you never
30. killed a fatted calf for me. But my younger
brother left the house and squandered all his
property with drunkards, and you have now
killed the calf for him.' And the father said:
31. 'You are always with me, and all mine is
32. yours; and you should not be offended, but
should be glad that your brother was dead and
has become alive, was lost and is found.'
Mk xii. 1.   "A master planted a garden, cultivated it,
arranged it, did everything so that the garden
might yield as much fruit as possible. And
he sent laborers into the garden, that they
might work there, and gather the fruit, and
pay him according to the agreement for the garden. (The master is the Father; the garden,
the world; the laborers, men. The Father
does no more than send His Son, the Son of
Man, into the world, that men may yield fruit
to the Father from the understanding of life
2. which He placed in them.) The time came
when the master sent a servant for the rents.
(The Father, without ceasing, tells men that
3. they must fulfil His will.) The laborers drove
away the messenger of the master with nothing,
and continued to live, imagining that the gar-

den was their own, and that they themselves, of their own will, were settled on it. (Men drive away from themselves the declaration of the will of the Father, and continue to live, each one for himself, imagining that they live for the joys of the fleshly life.)   Then the master sent one after another his chosen ones, then his son, to remind the laborers of their debt.   But the laborers quite lost their reason, and imagined that if they killed this son of the master, who reminded them that the garden was not theirs, they would be left quite in peace.   So they killed him.

"Thus men do not love even a reminder of the spirit which lives in them, and declares to them that it is eternal and they are not eternal; and they have killed, as far as they could, the consciousness of the spirit; they have wrapped in a cloth and buried in the ground the talent that was given them.

"What, then, is the master to do?   Nothing else than drive forth those laborers, and send others.

"What is the Father to do?   Sow until there shall be fruit.   And this He does.

"People have not understood and do not understand that the consciousness of the spirit which is in them, and which they hide because it troubles them, brings life to them through understanding it.   They reject that stone upon which everything rests.   And they who do not take as foundation the life of the spirit, do not enter into the kingdom of heaven, and do not receive life.   In order to have faith, and to receive life, it is necessary to understand one's position, and not to expect rewards."

Then the disciples said to Jesus: "Increase in us our faith.   Tell us that which will make us more strongly believe in the life of the spirit, that we may not regret the life of the flesh,

Mk. xii. 4,
6.

7.

8.

Mt. xxi. 40,
41.

42.

43.

Lk. xvii. 5

which must be given up wholly for the life of
the spirit.   For reward, you yourself say there
is none."

*k. xvii. 6.   And in answer to this, Jesus said to them :
" If you had such a faith as the faith that from
a birch seed there springs up a great tree ; if,
also, you believed that in you there is the germ,
the only germ, of the spirit whence springs up
the true life, you would not ask me to increase
in you your faith.

" Faith does not consist in believing something
wonderful, but faith consists in understanding
one's position, and wherein lies salvation.   If
you understand your position, you will not expect rewards, but will believe in that which is
intrusted to you.

7.   " When the master returns with the laborers
from the field, he does not seat the laborer at
8.   his table.   But he bids him see to the cattle,
and prepare his supper, and after this only
9.   says to the laborer : ' Sit down, drink and eat.'
The master will not thank the laborer for having done what he ought to do.   And the laborer, if he understands that he is a laborer,
is not offended, but works, believing that he
will receive his due.

10.   " And so you, also, must fulfil the will of
the Father, and think that we are worthless
laborers, having only done what we ought to
do, and not expect a reward, but be content
with receiving that which is due to you.

" There is no need to take care to believe
that there will be a reward, and life ; this cannot be otherwise; but there is need to take
care not to destroy this life, not to forget that
it is given us that we may bring forth its fruits,
and fulfil the will of the Father.

xii. 35,   " And therefore always be ready, like ser-
36.   vants awaiting a master, to answer him im-
37,   mediately when he comes.   The servants do
38.

not know when he will return, either early or
late, and they must always be ready. And
when they meet the master, they have fulfilled
his will, and it is well for them.

"So in life also. Always, every minute of the
present, you must live the life of the spirit, not
thinking of the past or the future, and not saying
to yourself : then or there I will do this or that.

"If the master knew when the thief would Lk. xii. 39.
come, he would not sleep; and so do you also
never sleep; because, to the life of the son of
man time is nothing; he lives only in the present, and does not know when is the beginning
or end of life.

"Our life is the same as that of a slave whom Mt. xxiv. 45,
the master has left as chief in his household. 46.
And well it is for that slave if he does the will
of the master always! But if he shall say, 48.
'The master will not soon return,' and shall forget the master's business, then the master will 50,
return unexpectedly, and will drive him out. 51.

"And so, be not downcast, but always live in Mk. xiii. 33.
the present by the spirit. For the life of the
spirit there is no time.

"Look to yourselves, so as not to weigh your- Lk. xxi. 34.
selves down, and not to blind yourselves with
drunkenness, gluttony, and cares; so as not
to let the time of salvation pass. The time of
salvation, like a web, is cast over all; it is
there always. And therefore always live the
life of the Son of Man.

"The kingdom of heaven is like this. Ten Mt. xxv. 1.
maidens went with lamps to meet the bridegroom.
Five were wise and five foolish. The foolish 2,
3.
ones took lamps but did not take oil; but the 4.
wise took lamps and a store of oil. While they 5.
waited for the bridegroom, they went to sleep.
When the bridegroom was approaching, the 6.
foolish maidens saw that they had little oil, and 7.
went to buy some; and while they were gone, 10.

the bridegroom came. And the wise maidens who had oil went in with him, and the doors were shut. Their business was only this, to meet the bridegroom with lights; and the five foolish ones forgot that it was important, not only that the lights should burn, but that they should burn in time. And in order that they might be burning when the bridegroom came, they must burn without stopping.

" Life is only for this, to exalt the Son of Man, and the Son of Man exists always. He is not in time; and therefore, in serving him, one must live without time, in the present alone.

Lk. xiii. 24.   " Therefore make efforts in the present to
25. enter into the life of the spirit. If you do not make these efforts you shall not enter. You will say: 'We said so and so.' But there will be no good works to show, and there will not
Mt. xvi. 27. be life. Because the Son of Man, the one true spirit of life, will appear in each man, as such man has acted for the Son of Man.

Mt. xxv. 32.   " Mankind is divided according to the way in which men serve the Son of Man. And by their works men shall be divided into two classes, as sheep are divided from goats in the flock. The one shall live, the other per‑ ish.

34.   " They who have served the Son of Man, they shall receive that which belonged to them from the beginning of the world, that life which they have kept. They have kept life by the fact that they have served the Son of Man. They have fed the hungry, clothed the naked, welcomed the stranger, visited the pris‑ oner. They have lived in the Son of Man, felt that he only is in all men, and therefore they have loved their neighbors.

" Whereas they who have not lived in the Son of Man, they have not served him, have not understood that he alone is in all, and therefore have not joined in him and have lost life in him, and have perished."

CHAPTER IX

TEMPTATIONS

The illusions of temporal life conceal from men the true life in the present

("𝔉𝔬𝔯𝔤𝔦𝔟𝔢 𝔲𝔰 𝔬𝔲𝔯 𝔡𝔢𝔟𝔱𝔰 𝔞𝔰 𝔴𝔢 𝔣𝔬𝔯𝔤𝔦𝔟𝔢 𝔬𝔲𝔯 𝔡𝔢𝔟𝔱𝔬𝔯𝔰")

ONCE, children were brought to Jesus. His disciples began to drive the children away. Jesus saw this being done, and was grieved, and said:— Mt. xix. 13.

14.

"You drive the children away without reason. They are better than any, because children all live after the Father's will. They are, indeed, already in the kingdom of heaven. You should not drive them away, but learn Lk. xviii. 17. from them; because, in order to live in the Father's will, you must live as children live. Children do not abuse one another, do not bear ill-will to people, do not commit adultery, do not swear by anything, do not resist evil, do not go to law with any one, acknowledge no difference between their own people and foreigners. Therefore are they better than grown people, and are in the kingdom of heaven. If Mt. xviii. 3. you do not refrain from all the temptations of the flesh, and become as children, you will not be in the kingdom of heaven.

"Only he who understands that children are better than we, because they do not break the Father's will, only he understands my teaching. And he who understands my teaching, Lk. ix. 48. he alone understands the Father's will. We Mt. xviii. 10. cannot despise children, because they are bet-

5.

ter than we, and their hearts are pure in the sight of the Father, and are always with Him.

Mt. xviii. 14. "And not one child perishes by the Father's will. They perish only as men entice them from the truth. And therefore it behooves us to take care of them, and not to entice them from the Father, and from true life.

"That man does ill who entices them from purity. To entice a child from good, to lead it into temptation, is as bad as to hang a mill-stone on its neck and throw it into the water. It is hard for it to swim to the surface; it is more likely to drown. It is as hard for a child to get out of temptation into which a grown-up man leads it.

7. "The world of men is unhappy only on account of temptations. Temptations are everywhere in the world, they always were and always will be; and man perishes from temptations.

8. "Therefore give up everything, sacrifice everything, if only you may not fall into temptation. A fox, if it fall into a trap, will wrench off its paw and go away, and the paw will heal and it will remain alive. Do you likewise. Give up everything, if only not to sink into temptation.

Lk. xvii. 3. "Beware of temptation under that first commandment; do not bear ill-will against men, when people offend you, and you would wish to be avenged on them.

Mt. xviii. 15. "If a man offend you, remember that he is the son of the same Father, and your brother. If he has offended you, go and persuade him of it face to face. If he listen to you, then you have the advantage, you will have found a new 16. brother. If he do not listen to you, then call to your aid two or three others who may per- Lk. xvii. 4. suade him. And if he repent, forgive him. And if he offend you seven times, and seven

times says, 'Forgive me,' then forgive him.
But if he does not listen, then tell the society   Mt. xviii. 17
of believers in my teaching, and if he listens
not to them, then forgive him, and have nothing to do with him.

"Because the kingdom of God is like this.   23.
A king began to settle with his tenants. And   24.
there was a man brought to him who owed him
a million, and had nothing to pay him with.
Then the king commanded to sell the man's   25.
estate, his wife, his children, and the man
himself. But the tenant began to beg mercy   26.
of the king. And the king was gracious to   27.
him, and pardoned all his debt. And now,   28.
this same tenant went home, and saw a peasant. This peasant owed him fifty shillings.
The king's tenant seized him, began to strangle
him, and said: 'Give me what you owe me.'
And the peasant fell at his feet, and said: 29.
'Have patience with me, I will pay you all.'
But the tenant showed him no mercy, and put   30.
the peasant into prison, to stay there until he
paid everything. Other peasants saw this,   31.
and went to the king, and told what the tenant had done. Then the king called the   32.
tenant, and said to him: 'Wicked creature,
I pardoned you all your debt, because you
prayed me. And you, also, should have shown   33.
mercy to your debtor, because I showed mercy
to you.' And the king became angry, and gave   34.
the tenant to be made to suffer, until he should
pay all his rent.

"Just so, the Father will do with you, if   35.
you do not forgive, from the bottom of your
heart, all those who are to blame in your sight.

"You know that if a quarrel arise with a   v. 25
man, it is better to make it up with him without going to the court. You know this, and
you act so because you know, should it go to
the court, you will lose more. Now, it is the

same with all malice. If you know that malice is a bad thing, and removes you from the Father, then get clear of malice as soon as possible, and make your peace.

Mt. xviii. 18. "You yourselves know that as you become bound on earth, so you will be before the Father. And as you free yourselves on earth, so you will be also free before the Father.

19. Understand that if two or three on earth are united in my teaching, everything they may desire they already have from my Father.

20. Because where two or three are joined in the name of the spirit in man, the spirit of man is living in them.

Mk. x. 2. "Beware also of temptation under the second commandment; the temptation for men to change their wives."

Mt. xix. 3. There once came to Jesus orthodox teachers, who, trying him, said: "May a man leave his wife?"

4. He said to them: "From the very beginning man was created male and female. This was

5. the will of the Father. And therefore a man leaves father and mother and cleaves to his wife. And husband and wife unite in one

6. body. So that the wife is the same for a man as his own flesh. Therefore man must not break the natural law of God, and separate

8. that which is united. According to your law of Moses, it is said that you may abandon a wife and take another; but this is untrue. According to the Father's will, this is not so,

9. and I tell you that he who casts off his wife drives into immorality both her, and him who shall have to do with her. And casting off his wife, a man breeds immorality in the world."

10. And the disciples said to Jesus: "It is too hard to be tied for life, whatever happens, to one wife. If that must be, it were better not to marry."

He said to them: "You may refrain from Mt. xix. 11
marriage, but you must understand what you
are about. If any one wishes to live without 12.
wife, let him be quite pure, and not approach
women; but he who loves women, let him
unite with one wife and not cast her off, and
not gaze upon others.

"Beware of temptation against the third
commandment; the temptation to force people
to fulfil obligations and to take oaths."

Once, tax-gatherers came to Peter, and asked xvii. 24.
him: "How about your teacher, does he pay
taxes?" Peter said: "No, he does not." 25.
And he went and told Jesus that he had been
stopped, and told that all were bound to pay
taxes.

Then Jesus said to him: "The king does
not take taxes of his sons; and moreover, men
are not bound to pay any one but the king. Is
this not so? Well, so it is with us. If we are
sons of God, then we are bound to no one but
God, and free from all obligations. And if they 27.
demand taxes of you, then pay. But do so,
not because it is your duty, but because you
may not resist evil. Otherwise resistance to
evil will cause a greater evil."

Another time, the orthodox joined with xxii. 16.
Cæsar's officials, and went to Jesus, to entrap
him in his words. They said to him: "You
teach every one according to the truth. Tell 17.
us, are we bound to pay taxes to Cæsar or
not?" Jesus understood that they wished to 18.
convict him of not acknowledging duty to
Cæsar. And he said to them: "Show me 19.
that with which you pay taxes to Cæsar."
They handed him a coin. He looked at the 20.
coin, and said: "What is this here? Whose
effigy and whose signature are these?" They
said: "Cæsar's." And he said: "Well then, 21.
pay Cæsar that which is Cæsar's, but that

which is God's, your soul, give to no one but to God." Money, goods, your labor, give everything to him who shall ask it of you. But your soul, give to none but God.

"Your orthodox teachers go about every-
Mt. xxiii. 15. where, and compel people to swear and vow that they will fulfil the law. But by this they only pervert people, and make them worse than before. It is impossible to promise with one's
16- body for one's soul. In your soul, God is;
22. therefore people cannot promise for God to men.

"Beware. Temptation under the fourth commandment is the temptation for men to judge and execute people, and call upon others to take part in these judgments and executions."
Lk. ix. 52. The disciples of Jesus once went into a village, and asked for a night's lodging; but they
53. were not admitted. Then the disciples went
54. to Jesus to complain, and said: "Let these
55. people be struck with lightning." Jesus said: "You still do not understand of what spirit you
56. are. I am teaching, not how to destroy, but how to save people."
xii. 13. Once a man came to Jesus, and said: "Bid my
14. brother give me my inheritance." Jesus said to him: "No one has made me judge over you, and I judge no one. And neither may you judge any one."
Jn. viii. 3. The orthodox once brought a woman to
4. Jesus, and said: "See, this woman was taken
5. in adultery. Now, by the law she should be stoned to death. What do you say?"
6. Jesus answered nothing, and waited for them
7. to bethink themselves. But they pressed him, and asked what he would adjudge to this woman. Then he said: "He among you who is without fault, let him be the first to cast a
8. stone at her." He said nothing more.
9. Then the orthodox looked within themselves,

and their consciences smote them; and they who were in front sought to get behind the others, and all went away. And Jesus re-   Jn. viii. 10 mained alone with the woman. He looked round, and saw that there was none else. "Well," said he to the woman, "has no one condemned you?" She said: "No one." Then   11. he said: "And I do not condemn you. Go, and henceforth sin no more."

Beware. Temptation against the fifth commandment is the temptation for men to consider themselves bound to do good only to their countrymen, and to consider foreigners as enemies.

A teacher of the law wished to try Jesus,   Lk.   x. 25. and said: "What am I to do in order to receive the true life?" Jesus said: "You know, — love   27. your Father, God, and him who is your brother through your Father, God; of whatever country he may be." And the teacher of the law said: 29. "This would be well, if there were not different nations; but as it is, how am I to love the enemies of my own people?"

And Jesus said: "There was a Jew who fell   30. into misfortune. He was beaten, robbed, and abandoned on the road. A Jewish priest went   31. by, glanced at the wounded man, and went on. A Jewish Levite passed, looked at the wounded   32. man, and also went by. But there came a man   33. of a foreign, hostile nation, a Samaritan. This Samaritan saw the Jew, and did not think of the fact that Jews have no esteem for the Samaritans, but pitied the poor Jew. He   34. washed and bound his wounds, and carried him on his ass to an inn, paid money for him   35. to the innkeeper, and promised to come again to pay for him. Thus shall you also behave toward foreign nations, toward those who hold you of no account and ruin you. Then you will receive true life."

Mt. xvi. 21. Jesus said : " The world loves its own, and hates God's people. Therefore men of the world — priests, preachers, officials — will harass those who shall fulfil the will of the Father. And I am going to Jerusalem, and shall be persecuted and killed. But my spirit cannot be killed, but will remain alive."

Mk viii. 32. Having heard that Jesus would be tortured and killed in Jerusalem, Peter was sad, and took Jesus by the hand, and said to him : "If so, 33. then you had better not go to Jerusalem." Then Jesus said to Peter : " Do not say this. What you say is temptation. If you fear tortures and death for me, this means that you are not thinking of that which is godly, of the spirit, but are thinking of what is worldly."

34. And having called the people and his disciples, Jesus said : " He who wishes to live according to my teaching, let him forsake his fleshly life, and let him be ready for all fleshly suffering ; because he who fears for his fleshly life, shall destroy the true life ; he who despises the fleshly life, shall save the true life."

Mt. xxii. 23. And they did not understand this, and certain materialists coming, he explained to all what is the meaning of the true life and the awakening from death.

The materialists said that after the fleshly 24. death there is no longer any life. They asked : " How can all rise from the dead ? If all were to rise, then in rising they could in no way have 25. life together. For instance, there were seven brothers among us. The first married and died. The wife was taken by the second brother and 28. he died, and she was taken by the third, who also died, and so on unto the seventh. Well now, how shall these seven brothers live with one wife if all arise from the dead ? "

Lk. xx. 34. Jesus said to them : " You either purposely confuse things, or you do not understand what

the awakening to life is.   Men in this present
life marry.   But they who shall earn everlast- Lk. xx. 35
ing life, and the awakening from death, do not
marry.   And that because they can no longer 36.
die, but are united with the Father.   In your Mt. xxii. 31.
writings, it is said that God said : ' I am the God 32.
of Abraham, Isaac, and Jacob.'   And this was
said when Abraham, Isaac, and Jacob had died
from among men.   It follows, that they who
have died from among men are alive to God.
If God is, and God does not die, then they who
are with God are always alive.   The awakening
from death is, to live in the will of the Father.
For the Father, there is no time ; therefore in
fulfilling the will of the Father, in joining Him,
man departs from time and death.''

When they heard this, the orthodox no longer 34.
knew what to devise to compel Jesus to hold
his tongue ; and together they began to question Jesus.   And one of the orthodox said : 35.
" Teacher, what, in your opinion, is the chief 36.
commandment in the whole law ? ''

The orthodox thought that Jesus would get
confused in the answer about the law.   But 37
Jesus said : " It is, to love the Lord with all
one's soul, in whose power we are.   From it the
second commandment follows, which is, to love
one's neighbor.   Because the same Lord is in 39.
him.   And this is the substance of all that is 40.
written in all your books.''

And Jesus said further : " In your opinion, 42.
what is Christ ? Is he some one's son ? ''   They
said : " In our opinion, Christ is the son of
David.''   Then he said to them : " How, then, 43.
does David call Christ his Lord?   Christ is
neither son of David, nor any one's son after
the flesh ; but Christ is that same Lord, our
Ruler, whom we know in ourselves as our life.
Christ is that understanding which is in us.''

And Jesus said : " See, beware of the leaven Lk. xii. 1

of orthodox teachers. And beware of the leaven
of the materialists and of the leaven of the gov-
Lk. xii. 5 ernment. But most of all, beware of the leaven
of the self-styled 'orthodox,' because in them
is the chief stumbling-block."

xx. 45. And when the people understood of what he
46. was speaking, he repeated: "Most of all, beware of the teaching of the scholars, of the
Mt. xxiii. 2. self-called 'orthodox.' Beware of them, because they have taken the place of the prophets
who declared the will of God to the people.
They have perversely assumed authority to
preach to the people the will of God. They
preach words, and do nothing. And the result
3. is that they no more than say: 'Do this and
that.' And there is no further result, because
4. they do nothing good, but only talk. And they
tell people to do what is impossible to be done,
5. and they themselves do nothing. They only
labor to keep the teaching in their own hands;
and with this aim they strive to appear imposing; they dress themselves up and exalt them-
8. selves. Know, therefore, that no one should
13. call himself teacher and leader. But the self-
styled orthodox are called teachers, and by this
very thing they hinder you from entering into
the kingdom of heaven, where they themselves
15. do not enter. These orthodox think that people may be brought to God by exterior rites
16. and pledges. Like blind men, they do not see
that the outside show means nothing; that all
23. depends upon the soul of man. They do the
easiest thing, the external thing; that which is
needful and difficult — love, compassion, truth
28. — they leave undone. It suffices them to be
only outwardly in the law, and to bring others
27. outwardly to the law. And therefore they, like
painted coffins, outwardly look clean, but are
30. an abomination within. They outwardly honor
31. the holy martyrs. But in very deed they are the

same as those who torture and kill the saints. They were before, and are now, the enemies of all good. From them comes all the evil in the world; because they hide the good, and instead of it uphold evil. Most of all to Mk iii. 28 be feared, therefore, are self-called teachers. Because you yourselves know every mistake may be made good. But if people are mis- 29 taken as to what good is, this mistake can never be set right. And this is precisely the condition of self-called leaders."

And Jesus said: "I wished, here in Jeru- Mt. xxiii. 37. salem, to join all men in one understanding of true happiness; but the people here are only capable of putting to death the teachers of good. And therefore they will remain the 38. same godless people as they were, and will not know the true God; until they shall lovingly 39. welcome the understanding of God." And xxiv. 1. Jesus went away from the temple.

Then his disciples said to him: "But what will happen to this temple of God, with all its embellishments which people have brought into it, to give to God." And Jesus said: "I 2. tell you truly, the whole of this temple, with all its embellishments, shall be destroyed, and nothing shall remain of it. There is one temple of God; that is, the hearts of men when they love each other."

And they asked him: "When shall there be 3. such a temple?" And Jesus said to them: 4. "That will not be soon. People will yet long be deceived in the name of my teaching, and wars and rebellions will be the result. And 12. there will be great lawlessness, and little love. But when the true teaching shall spread among 14 all men, then will be the end of evil and temptations."

CHAPTER X

THE WARFARE WITH TEMPTATION

Therefore, not to fall by temptation, we must, at every moment of life, be at one with the Father

("𝕷𝔢𝔞𝔡 𝔲𝔰 𝔫𝔬𝔱 𝔦𝔫𝔱𝔬 𝔱𝔢𝔪𝔭𝔱𝔞𝔱𝔦𝔬𝔫")

Lk. xi. 53. AFTER this, the orthodox chief priests began to do all they could to lay traps for Jesus, in **Jn. xi. 47.** some way or other to destroy him. They gath-**48.** ered in council, and began to consider. They said: "This man must somehow or other be put an end to. He so proves his teaching that, if he be left alone, all will believe in him, and cast off our belief. Already half of the people believe in him. But if the Jews believe in his teaching, that all men are sons of one Father, and brothers, and that there is nothing in our Hebrew people different from other peoples, then the Romans will completely overwhelm us, and the Hebrew kingdom will be no more."

Lk. xix. 47. And the orthodox high priest and learned men for long counseled together, and could **48.** not think what to do with Jesus. They could not make up their minds to kill him.

Jn. xi. 49. Then one of them, Caiaphas, the chief priest of that year, thought of the following device. **50.** He said to the others: "You must remember this: it is expedient to kill one man, that the whole people may not perish. If we leave this man alone, the people will perish; this I declare to you. Therefore it is better to kill **52.** Jesus. Even if the people do not perish, they will nevertheless go astray, departing from the one belief, if we do not kill Jesus. Therefore it is better to kill Jesus."

53. And when Caiaphas said this, they resolved

that there was no need to discuss, but that Jesus must be killed without fail.

They would have taken Jesus at once and killed him, but he withdrew from them into the desert. But at this time the feast of the Passover was approaching, when a great multitude always gathered in Jerusalem. And the orthodox high priests reckoned upon Jesus coming with the people to the feast. And they made known to the people that if any one should see Jesus he should bring him to them. Jn. xi. 54

55

56

57.

And it so happened that, six days before the Passover, Jesus said to his disciples: " Let us go to Jerusalem." And he went with them. xii. 1.
xi. 7.

And the disciples said to him: " Do not go into Jerusalem. The high priests have resolved now to stone you to death. If you come they will kill you." 8.

Jesus said to them: " I can fear nothing, because I live in the light of understanding. And as every man, that he may not stumble, walks by day and not by night, so every man, that he may doubt nothing and fear nothing, must live by this understanding. Only he doubts and fears who lives by the flesh; but he who lives by understanding, for him there is nothing doubtful or fearful." 9.

10.

And Jesus came to the village of Bethany, near Jerusalem, and to the house of Martha and Mary which was there. xii. 1.

Early in the morning Jesus went into Jerusalem. There was a great crowd for the feast. And when they recognized Jesus, they surrounded him, tore branches from the trees, and threw their clothes before him on the road, and all shouted: " Here is our true king, he who has taught us the true God." 12.

13.

Jesus sat upon an ass's foal, riding, and the people ran before him and shouted; thus he rode into Jerusalem. And when he had thus 14.

Mt. xxi. 10

ridden into the town, the whole people were
Mt. xxi. 11. excited, and asked: "Who is he?" They who
knew him answered: "Jesus, the prophet of
Nazareth, in Galilee."

Mk. xi. 15. And Jesus went into the temple, and again
drove out thence all the buyers and sellers.

Jn. xii. 19. And the orthodox high priests saw all this,
and said to each other: "See what this man
is doing. The whole people are following
him."

Mk. xi. 18. But they did not dare to take him straight
from among the people, because they saw that
the people were gathering round him, and they
bethought them how to take him by cunning.

Jn. xii. 20. Meanwhile Jesus was in the temple, and
taught the people. Among the people, besides Jews, there were Greeks and heathen.
The Greeks heard of the teaching of Jesus, and
understood his teaching in this way, namely,
that he taught the truth, not only to Hebrews
21. but to all men. Therefore they wished to be
also his disciples, and spoke about this to
22. Philip. And Philip told this to Andrew.

These two disciples feared to bring Jesus
together with the Greeks. They were afraid
lest the people should be angry with Jesus,
because he did not recognize any difference
between Hebrews and other nations, and they
long wavered about telling this to Jesus; but
afterward both together told him, and hearing
that the Greeks wished to be his followers,
Jesus was troubled. He knew that the people
hated him because he made no difference
between the Hebrews and the heathen, but
acknowledged himself to be the same as the
heathen.

23. He said: "The hour is come to explain
what I understand by the Son of Man, though
I perish because, in explaining this, I destroy
distinction between Jews and heathen. I must

speak the truth. A grain of wheat will only Jn. xii. 24
bring forth fruit when it itself perishes. He 25
who loves his fleshly life loses the true life, and
he who despises the fleshly life keeps it for the
everlasting life. He who wishes to follow my
teaching, let him do as I do. And he who 26.
does as I do shall be rewarded by my Father.
My soul is now wrestling. Shall I surrender 27.
myself to the compromises of temporary life,
or fulfil the will of the Father, now, at this
hour? And what then? Surely now, when
this hour is come in which I am living, I shall
not say: 'Father, save me from that which I
should do.' I cannot say this for the sake of
my life. And therefore I say: 'Father, show 28.
yourself in me.'"

And Jesus said: "Henceforth the present 31.
society of men is condemned to destruction.
From now that which rules this world shall be
destroyed. And when the Son of Man shall 32.
be exalted above the earthly life, then shall
he unite all in one."

Then the Jews said to him: "We under- 34.
stand from the law what the everlasting Christ
is; but why do you say that the Son of Man
shall be exalted? What is the meaning of
exalting the Son of Man?"

To this Jesus answered: "To exalt the 35.
Son of Man, means to live by the life of understanding that is in you. To exalt the Son 36.
of Man above that which is earthly, means to
believe in the light while there is light, in
order to be a son of understanding.

"He who believes in my teaching believes 44.
not in me, but in that spirit which gave life
to the world. And he who understands my 45.
teaching, understands that spirit which gave
life to the world. But if any one hears my 47.
words and does not fulfil them, it is not I who
blame him, seeing that I came, not to accuse,

Jn. xii. 48. but to save. He who does not accept my words is accused, not by my teaching, but by the understanding which is in himself. This
49. it is which accuses him. I did not speak of myself, but said what my Father, the living
50. spirit in me, suggested to me. That which I say, the spirit of understanding has told me, and that which I teach is the true life."

36. And having said this, Jesus went away, and again hid from the chief priests.

42. And of those who heard these words of Jesus, many of the powerful and wealthy people believed, but were afraid to acknowledge it to the chief priests, because not one of these priests believed and acknowledged it.
43. They were accustomed to judge according to man, and not according to God.

Mt. xxvi. 3. After Jesus had hidden, the high priests and the elders again met in the court of Caiaphas.
4. And they began to plan how to take Jesus
5. unknown to the people, for they were afraid
14. to seize him openly. And there came to their council one of the first twelve disciples of
15. Jesus, Judas Iscariot, who said: "If you wish to take Jesus secretly, so that the people may not see, I will find a time when there will be few people with him, and will show you where he is; and then take him. But what will you give me for this?" They promised him for
16. this thirty silver coins. He agreed; and from that time began to seek an opportunity to bring the chief priests upon Jesus, in order to take him.

17. Meanwhile Jesus withdrew from the people, and with him were only his disciples. When the first feast of unleavened bread approached, the disciples said to Jesus: "Where, then, shall
18. we keep the Passover?" And Jesus said: "Go into some village, and enter some one's house, and say that we have not time to prepare the

feast, and ask him to admit us to celebrate the
Passover." And the disciples did so; they   Mt. xxvi. 19
asked a man in the village, and he invited them
in. And they came and sat down to the table,   20
Jesus and the twelve disciples, Judas among
them.

Jesus knew that Judas Iscariot had already   Jn.   xiii. 11
promised to betray him to death, but he did
not accuse Judas for this, or show him ill-will,
but as in all his life he taught his disciples
love, so even now he only reproached Judas
lovingly. When they all twelve were seated   Mt. xxvi. 21.
at table, he looked at them, and said: "Among   Mk. xiv. 18.
you sits he who has betrayed me. Yes, he who   Mt. xxvi. 23.
eats and drinks with me shall also destroy me."
And he said nothing more, so that they did not
know of whom he spoke, and they began to sup.

When they began to eat, Jesus took a loaf   26.
and broke it into twelve parts, and gave each
of the disciples a piece, and said : ."Take and
eat, this is my body." And he then filled a   27.
cup with wine, handed it to the disciples, and
said : "Drink, all of you, of this cup." And
when they had all drunk, he said: "This is
my blood. I shed it that people may know   28.
my will, to forgive others their sins. For I   Lk. xxii. 18
shall soon die, and be no more with you in this
world, but shall join you only in the kingdom
of heaven."

After this, Jesus got up from the table, girt   Jn. xiii. 4.
himself with a towel, took a ewer of water,   5.
and began to wash the feet of all the disciples.
And he came to Peter; and Peter said: "But   6
why will you wash my feet?" Jesus said to   7
him: "It seems strange to you that I should
wash your feet; but you will know soon why I
do this. Though you are clean, yet not all of   10
you are so, but among you is my betrayer, to
whom I gave, with my own hand, bread and
wine, and whose feet I wish to wash."

Jn. xiii. 12. When Jesus had washed all their feet, he again sat down, and said: "Do you understand 14. why I did this? It was so that you always may do the same for each other. I, your teacher, do this, that you may know how to 17. behave toward those who do you evil. If you have understood this, and will do it, then you will 18. be happy. When I said that one of you will betray me, I did not speak of all of you, because only a single one of you, whose feet I washed, and who ate bread with me, will betray me."

21. And having said this, Jesus was troubled in spirit, and yet again said: "Yes, yes, one of you will betray me."

22. And again the disciples began to look round at each other, not knowing of whom he spoke. 23. One disciple sat near to Jesus, and Simon 24. Peter signed to him in a way to ask who 25. the betrayer was. The disciple asked. And 26. Jesus said: "I will soak a piece of bread, and give it to him: and he to whom I shall give it 27. is my betrayer." And he gave the bread to Judas Iscariot, and said to him: "What you 30. wish to do, do quickly." Then Judas understood that he must go out, and as soon as he had taken the bread he forthwith went out. And it was impossible to follow him, as it was night.

31. And when Judas was gone out, Jesus said: "It is now clear to you what the Son of Man is. It is now clear to you that in him God is, to make him as blessed as God Himself.

33. "Children! I have not long now to be with you. Do not equivocate over my teaching, as I said to the orthodox, but do that which I do. 34. I give you this, a new commandment. As I always, and to the end, have loved you all, do you always, and to the end, love each other. 35. By this only will you be distinguished. Seek to be only thus distinguished from other people. Love one another."

And after this, they went to the Mount of Olives. Mt. xxvi. 30

And on the way Jesus said to them: "See, the time is coming when that shall happen which is written, the shepherd shall be killed, and all the sheep shall be scattered. And to-night this shall happen. I shall be taken, and you will all abandon me, and scatter." 31.

Peter said to him in answer: "Even if all shall be frightened, and scatter, I will not deny you. I am ready for prison and for death with you." 33.

And Jesus said to him: "But I tell you that this very night, before cock-crow, after I have been taken, you will deny me, not once, but thrice." 34.

But Peter said that he would not deny him; and the other disciples averred the same. 35.

Then Jesus said to the disciples: "Before, neither I nor you had need of anything. You went without wallet and without change of shoes, and I so bade you do. But now, if I am accounted an outlaw, we can no longer do so, but we must be furnished with everything, and with swords, that we may not perish in vain." Lk. xxii. 35. 36.

And the disciples said: "See, we have two swords." 38.

Jesus said: "It is well."

And having said this, Jesus went with the followers into the garden of Gethsemane. Coming into the garden, he said: "Wait you here, but I wish to pray." Mt. xxvi. 36.
Jn. xviii. 1.

And while near to Peter and the two brothers, sons of Zebedee, he began to feel weary and sad, and he said to them: "I feel very sad and my soul is full of the anguish before death. Wait here, and be not cast down as I am." Mt. xxvi. 37. 38.

And he went off a little way, lay on the ground on his face, and began to pray, and said: "My 39

Father, the Spirit! Let it be not as I will, which is that I should not die, but let it be as Thou wilt. Let me die, but for Thee, as a spirit, all is possible; let it be that I may not fear death, that I may escape the temptation of the flesh."

Mt. xxvi. 40.   And then he arose, went up to the disciples, and saw that they were cast down. And he said to them: "How is it you have not strength for one hour to keep up your spirit even as I!

41.   Keep up your spirit, so as not to fall into the temptation of the flesh. The spirit is strong, the flesh is weak."

42.   And again Jesus went away from them, and again began to pray, and said: "Father, if I must suffer, must die, and am about to die, then

43.   so let it be. Let Thy will be done." And having said this, he again went up to the disciples, and saw that they were still more cast down, and ready to weep.

44.   And he again went away from them, and the third time said: "Father, let Thy will be done."

45.   Then he returned to the disciples, and said to them: "Now be easy, and be calm, because it is now decided that I shall give myself into the hands of worldly men."

CHAPTER XI

THE FAREWELL DISCOURSE

The self-life is an illusion which comes through the flesh, an evil. The true life is the life common to all men

("Deliver us from evil")

Jn. xiii. 36.   AND Peter said to Jesus: "Whither are you going?"

Jesus answered: "You will not have the strength now to go whither I am going; but afterward you will go the same way."

And Peter said : " Why do you think that I Jn. xiii. 37
have not the strength now to follow whither you
go ? I will give up my life for you."

And Jesus said : " You say that you will give 38.
up your life for me, and yet even before cock-
crow you shall deny me thrice." And Jesus xiv. 1.
said to the disciples : " Be not troubled and be
not afraid, but believe in the true God of life,
and in my teaching.

"The life of the Father is not only that which 2.
is on earth, but there is another life also. If 3.
there were only such a life as the life here, I
would say to you, that when I die I shall go
into Abraham's bosom, and make ready a place
there for you, and I shall come and take you,
and we shall together live happily in Abraham's
bosom. But I point out to you only the direc- 4.
tion to life."

Thomas said : " But we do not know whither 5.
you go, and therefore we cannot know the way.
We want to know what there will be after death."

Jesus said : " I cannot show you what will be 6.
there ; my teaching is the way, and the truth,
and the life. And it is impossible to be joined
with the Father of life otherwise than through
my teaching. If you fulfil my teaching, you 7.
shall know the Father."

Philip said : "But who is the Father ? " 8.

And Jesus said : "The Father is He who gives 9.
life. I have fulfilled the will of the Father, and
therefore by my life you may know wherein is
the will of the Father. I live by the Father, 10.
and the Father lives in me. All that I say and 11.
do, I do by the will of the Father. My teaching
is, that I am in the Father and the Father is in
me. If you do not understand my teaching, yet
you see me and my works. And therefore you
may understand what the Father is. And you 12.
know that he who shall follow my teaching may
do the same as I ; and yet more, because I shall

Jn xiv. 13. die, but he will still live. He who shall live according to my teaching, shall have all that he wishes, because then the Son will be one with **14.** the Father. Whatever you may wish that accords with my teaching, all that you shall **15.** have. But for this you must love my teaching. **16.** My teaching will give you, in my place, an in-**17.** tercessor and comforter. This comforter will be the consciousness of truth, which worldly men do not understand ; but you will know it in your-**18.** selves. You never will be alone, if the spirit of **19.** my teaching is with you. I shall die, and worldly men will not see me ; but you will see me because my teaching lives and you will live **20.** by it. And then, if my teaching shall be in you, you will understand that I am in the Father and **21.** the Father in me. He who shall fulfil my teach-ing, shall feel in himself the Father ; and in him my spirit shall live."

22. And Judas, not Iscariot, but another, said to him : " But why, then, may not all live by the spirit of truth ? "

23. Jesus said in answer : " Only he who fulfils my teaching, only him the Father loves, and in **24.** him only can my spirit abide. He who does not fulfil my teaching, him my Father cannot love, because this teaching is not mine, but the **25.** Father's. This is all that I can tell you now. **26.** But my spirit, the spirit of truth, which shall take up its abode in you after I am gone, shall reveal to you all, and you shall recall and understand much of that which I have told **27.** you. So that you may always be calm in spirit, not with that worldly calm which men of the world seek, but with that calm of spirit in **28.** which we no longer fear anything. On this account, if you fulfil my teaching, you have no reason to grieve over my death. I, as the spirit of truth, will come to you, and, together with the knowledge of the Father, will take up my abode in your heart. If you fulfil my teaching, then you must rejoice, because instead of me you will have the Father with you in your heart, and this is better for you.

" My teaching is the tree of life. The Father Jn. xv. 1. is He who tends the tree. He prunes and 2. cherishes those branches upon which there is fruit, that they may yield more. Keep my 4. teaching of life, and life will be in you. And as a shoot lives not of itself, but out of the tree, so do you live by my teaching. My 5. teaching is the tree, you are the shoots. He who lives by my teaching of life yields much fruit; and without my teaching there is no life. He who does not live by my teaching 6. withers and dies; and the dry branches are cut off and burnt.

" If you will live by my teaching, and fulfil it, 7. then you shall have all that you desire. Be- 8. cause the will of the Father is, that you may live the true life and have that which you desire. As the Father gave me happiness, so I 9. give you happiness. Hold to this happiness. I am living, because the Father loves me and 10. I love the Father; do you also live by the same love. If you will live by this, you shall 11. be blessed.

" My commandment is, that you love one 12. another as I have loved you. There is no 13. greater love than to sacrifice one's life for the love of one's own, as I have done.

" You are my equals, if you do that which I 14. have taught you. I do not hold you as slaves, 15. to whom orders are given, but as equals; because I have made clear to you all that I have known of the Father. You do not, of your 16. own will, choose my teaching; but because I have pointed out to you that only truth by which you will live, and from which you will have all that you wish.

Jn. xv. 17.   " The teaching is summed up in this — Love one another.

18.   " If the world should hate you, then do not
19. wonder; it hates my teaching. If you were at one with the world, it would love you. But I have severed you from the world, and for
20. that it will hate you. If they persecuted me,
21. they will persecute you also. They will do all this, because they do not know the true
22. God. I explained to them, but they did not
23. wish to hear me. They did not understand my teaching, because they did not under-
24. stand the Father. They saw my life, and my
25. life showed them their error. And for this
26. they still more hated me. The spirit of truth which shall come to you will confirm this
27. to you. And you will accept it. I tell you
xvi. 1. this beforehand, so that you may not be deceived when persecutions shall be upon
2. you. You shall be made outcasts; men shall think that in killing you they do God's pleas-
3. ure. All this they cannot help doing, be- cause they understand neither my teaching
4. nor the true God. All this I tell you before- hand, so that you may not wonder when it comes about.

5.   "Well then, I now go away to that Spirit which sent me ; and now you understand, you
6. need not ask me whither I go. But before, you were grieved that I did not tell you whither, to what place, I depart.

7.   " But I tell you truly that it is well for you that I am going. If I do not die, the spirit of truth will not appear to you, but if I die, it
8. will take up its abode in you. It will take up its abode in you, and it will be clear to you where untruth is, where truth is,
9. and how to make decision. Untruth, in that people do not believe in the life of the
10. spirit. Truth, in that I am one with the

Father. Decision, in that the power of Jn. xvi. 11
the fleshly life is at an end.

"I would say yet much more to you, but it 12.
is difficult for you to understand. But when 13.
the spirit of truth dwells in you, it will show
you the whole truth, because it will tell you,
not a new thing of its own, but that which is
of God; and it will show you the way in all
concerns of life. It also will be from the 15.
Father, as I am from the Father; therefore it
also will tell you the same as I tell you.

"But when I, the spirit of truth, shall be in 16.
you, you will not always see me. Sometimes
you will, and sometimes you will not, hear
me."

And the disciples said one to another: 17.
"What does he mean when he says: 'Sometimes you will see me, sometimes you will not
see me.' What means this, 'Sometimes you 18.
will, sometimes you will not'?"

Jesus said to them: "Do you not under- 19.
stand what this means, 'Sometimes you will,
sometimes you will not, see me'? You know 20.
how it always is in the world, that some are
sad and grieved, while others rejoice. And
you will grieve, but your grief will pass into
joy. A woman, when she bears, grieves while 21.
she is in the pangs of childbirth; but when
that is ended, she does not remember the pangs,
for joy that a man is born into the world. And 22.
so you will grieve; anon you will see me, the
spirit of truth will enter into you, and your
grief will be turned into joy. Then you will 23.
no longer ask anything of me, because you will
have all that you wish. Then all which one of
you desires in the spirit, all that he will have
from his Father.

"You formerly asked for nothing for the 24
spirit; but now ask what you will for the
spirit, and you will have all; so that your

Jn. xvi. 25. bliss will be full.   Now I, as a man, cannot
tell you this clearly in words, but when I, as
the spirit of truth, shall live in you, I will
proclaim to you clearly about the Father.

26. Then it will not be I who will give you all you
ask of the Father in the name of the spirit.

27. But the Father will Himself give, because He
loves you for having received my teaching.

28. You have understood that understanding proceeds from the Father into the world and returns from the world to the Father."

29. Then the disciples said to Jesus: "Now
we have understood everything, and have

30. nothing more to ask, we believe that you are
from God."

33. And Jesus said: "All that I have said to
you is in order that you may have confidence
and rest in my teaching.   Whatever ills may
befall you in the world, fear nothing: my
teaching will conquer the world."

xvii. 1. After this, Jesus raised his eyes to heaven,
and said:

"My Father!   Thou hast given Thy Son
the freedom of life in order that he may re-

3. ceive the true life.   Life is the knowledge of
the true God of the understanding, Who is

6. discovered to me.   I have discovered Thee to

4. men on earth; I have done that work which
Thou hast bidden me do.   I have shown Thy

6. being to men on earth.   They were Thine
before, but by Thy will I have discovered to

7. them the truth, and they know Thee.   They
8. have understood that all they have, their life,
is from Thee only, and that I have taught
them, not of myself, but as proceeding, I with

9. them, from Thee.   But I pray to Thee for

10, those who acknowledge Thee.   They have
11. understood that all that I have is Thine, and
all that is Thine is mine.   I am no longer in the
world, for I return to Thee; but they are in

the world, and therefore I pray Thee, Father, to preserve in them Thy understanding. I do Jn. xvii. 15 not pray Thee to remove them from the world, but to free them from evil; to confirm them 17. in Thy truth. Thy understanding is the truth. 18. My Father! I wish them to be as I am; to 21. understand as I do, that the true life began before the beginning of the world. That they should all be one; as Thou, Father, art in me, and I in Thee, so they may also be one in me. I in them, Thou in me, so that all may be one; 23. so that all men may understand they are not self-created, but that Thou, in love, hast sent them into the world as Thou didst send me. Father of truth! the world did not know Thee, 25 but I knew Thee, and they have known Thee through me. And I have made plain to them 26. what Thou art. Thou art in me, that the love with which Thou hast loved me may be in them also. Thou gavest them life, and therefore didst love them. I have taught them to know this, and to love Thee; so that Thy love might be returned from them to Thee."

CHAPTER XII

THE VICTORY OF THE SPIRIT OVER THE FLESH

Therefore, for him who lives, not the self-life, but a common life in the will of the Father, there is no death. Bodily death is for him union with the Father

("Thine is the kingdom, power, and glory")

AFTER this, Jesus said: "Now arise, and Mt. xxvi. 46 let us go; already he is coming who will betray me."
And he had hardly said this, when suddenly 47 Judas, one of the twelve disciples, appeared, and with him a great throng of people with

Mt. xxvi. 48. sticks and swords. Judas said to them: " I will bring you where he and his followers are. and so that you may know him among them all, he whom I shall first kiss, that is he."

49. And he straightway went up to Jesus, and said: "Hail, teacher!" and kissed him.

50. And Jesus said to him: "Friend, why are you here?"

Then the guard surrounded Jesus, and wished to take him.

51. And Peter snatched the sword from the high priest's servant, and slashed the man's ear.

52. But Jesus said: "You must not oppose evil. Cease." And he said to Peter: "Return the sword to him from whom you took it; he who shall draw the sword, shall perish with the sword."

55. And after this, Jesus turned to the crowd, and said: "Why have you come out against me, as against a robber, with arms? I was every day among you in the temple, and taught

Lk. xxii. 53. you, and you did not take me. But now is your hour, and the power of darkness."

Mt. xxvi. 56. Then, having seen that he was taken, all the disciples ran away.

Jn. xviii. 12. And the officer ordered the soldiers to take Jesus, and bind him. The soldiers bound him,

13. and took him first to Annas. This was the father-in-law of Caiaphas, and Caiaphas was the high priest for that year, and lived in the

14. same house with Annas. This was the same Caiaphas who planned how to destroy Jesus. He held that it was good for the sake of the people to destroy Jesus, because, if that were not done, it would be worse for the whole peo-

Mk. xiv. 53. ple. And they took Jesus to the house where this high priest lived.

Mt. xxvi. 58. When they had brought Jesus thither, one of his disciples, Peter, followed him from afar, and watched where they were taking him. When they brought Jesus into the court of the high priest, Peter went in also, to see how all would end. And a girl in the yard saw Peter, Mt. xxvi. 69 and said to him: "You, also, were with Jesus of Galilee." Then Peter was afraid that they 70. would accuse him also, and he said aloud before all the people: "I do not know what you are talking about." Afterward, when they 71. had taken Jesus into the house, Peter also entered the hall, with the people. In the hall, a woman was warming herself at the fire, and Peter approached. The woman looked at Peter, and said to the people : " See, this man is likely to have been with Jesus of Nazareth." Peter 72. was still more frightened, and swore that he never was with him, and did not even know what kind of a man Jesus was. A little while 73. after, the people came up to Peter, and said: "It is quite clear that you also were among the disturbers. By your speech one may know that you are from Galilee." Then Peter began to 74. swear, and aver that he had never known or seen Jesus.

And he had hardly said this, when the cock 75. crew. And Peter remembered those words which Jesus had said to him, when Peter swore that if all denied Jesus, he would not deny him: " Before the cock crow this night, you will deny me thrice." And Peter went out, and cried bitterly. Jesus had prayed that he might not thus fall into temptation. He had fallen into one temptation, that of strife, when he began to defend Jesus; and into another temptation, the fear of death, when he denied Jesus.

And there gathered to the high priest, the Mk xiv. 53. orthodox chief priests, assistants, and officials. And when all were assembled, they brought in Jn. xviii. 19 Jesus; and the chief priests asked him, what was his teaching, and who were his followers.

Jn. xviii. 20.   And Jesus answered: "I always said all I
had to say before everybody openly, and so
I speak now; I concealed nothing from any
21.   one, and I conceal nothing now.   But about
what do you question me?   Question those
who heard and understood my teaching.   They
will tell you."

22.   When Jesus had said this, one of the high
priest's servants struck him in the face, and
said: "To whom are you speaking?   Is this
the way to answer the high priest?"

23.   Jesus said: "If I spoke ill, say what I spoke
ill.   But if I said nothing ill, then there is no
cause to beat me."

Mt. xxvi. 59.   The orthodox chief priests strove to accuse
Jesus, and at first did not find any proofs against
him for which it was possible to condemn him.

60,   Afterward they found two witnesses.   These
61.   said about Jesus: "We ourselves heard how
this man said: 'I will destroy this temple of
yours made with hands, and in three days will
build up another temple to God, not made with
59.   hands.'"   But this evidence, also, was not
62.   enough to condemn him.   And therefore the
high priest called up Jesus, and said: "Why
do you not answer their evidence?"

63.   Jesus held his tongue, saying nothing.   Then
the high priest said to him: "Well, say then,
Are you the Christ, and of God?"

64.   Jesus answered him, and said: "Yes, I am
the Christ, and of God.   You yourselves will
now see that the Son of Man is made like God."

65.   Then the high priest cried out: "You blas-
pheme!   Now we do not want any evidence.
We all hear, now, that you are a blasphemer."

66.   And the high priest turned to the assembly,
and said: "You have yourselves heard that
he blasphemes God.   To what do you sentence
him for this?"

And all said: "We sentence him to death."

Then all the people, and the guards, fell _{Mt. xxvi. 67} upon Jesus, and began to spit in his face, to strike him on the cheeks, and to tear at him. They covered his eyes, hit him in the face, and asked: "Now, prophet, guess who it was that hit you?"

But Jesus held his peace.

Having abused him, they took him, bound, to Pontius Pilate. And they brought him into the court.

Pilate, the governor, came out to them and asked: "Of what do you accuse this man?"

They said: "This man is doing wrong, so we have brought him to you."

And Pilate said to them: "But if he does wrong, then judge him yourselves according to your law."

And they said: "We have brought him to you that you might execute him, for we are not allowed to kill any one."

And so that happened which Jesus expected. He said that one must be ready to die on the cross at the hands of the Romans, more likely than at the hands of the Jews.

And when Pilate asked, whereof they accused him, they said, that he was guilty of stirring up the people, and that he forbade the payment of taxes to Cæsar, and that he set up himself as Christ and king.

Pilate listened to them, and bade Jesus be brought to him in the court. When Jesus came in, Pilate said to him: "So you are king of the Jews?"

Jesus said to him: "Do you really suppose that I am a king, or are you repeating only that which others have told you?"

Pilate said: "I am not a Jew, therefore you cannot be my king, but your people have brought you to me. What kind of a man are you?"

Jn. xviii 36. Jesus answered: "I am a king; but my kingdom is not an earthly one. If I were an earthly king, my subjects would fight for me, and would not yield to the high priests. But as it is, you see that my kingdom is not an earthly one."

37. Pilate said to this: "But yet, do you not consider yourself a king?" Jesus said: "Not only I, but you also, cannot but consider me a king. For I only teach, in order to discover to all the truth of the kingdom of heaven. And every one who lives by the truth, is a king."

38. Pilate said: "You spoke of truth. What is truth?"

And having said this, he turned, and went to the chief priests. He went out and said to them: "In my opinion, this man has done no wrong."

Mk. xv. 3. But the chief priests insisted upon their opinion, and said that he was doing much evil, and stirring up the people, and had raised the whole of Judea right from Galilee.

4. Then Pilate, in the presence of the chief priests, began to question Jesus. But Jesus did not answer. Pilate then said to him: "Do you hear of what they accuse you? Why do you not justify yourself?"

5. But Jesus still held his tongue, and said not another word, so that Pilate wondered at him.

Lk. xxiii. 6. Pilate remembered that Galilee was in the power of King Herod, and asked: "Ah! he is from Galilee?" They answered: "Yes."

7. Then he said: "If he is from Galilee, then he is under the authority of Herod, and I will send him to him." Herod was then in Jerusalem, and Pilate, in order to rid himself, sent Jesus to Herod.

8. When they brought Jesus to Herod, Herod was very glad to see him. He had heard much

of him, and wished to know what kind of man
he was. So he called Jesus to him, and began   Lk. xxiii. 9
to question him about all he wished to know.
But Jesus answered him nothing. And the   10
chief priests and teachers, just as with Pilate,
so before Herod, vehemently accused Jesus,
and said that he was a rioter. And Herod   11
deemed Jesus an empty fellow, and to mock
him, bade them clothe him in red, and send
him back to Pilate. Herod was pleased at   12
Pilate's showing respect to him, by sending
Jesus for his judgment, and on this account
they became friends, whereas formerly they
had been at variance.

Now, when they brought Jesus again to   13.
Pilate, Pilate called back the chief priests
and Jewish authorities, and said to them:
"You brought this man to me for stirring   14.
up the people, and I have examined him
before you, and do not see that he is a rioter.
I sent him with you to Herod, and now, see,   15.
— nothing wrong is found in him. And, in
my opinion, there is no cause to punish him
with death. Had you not better punish him
and let him go?"

But when the chief priests heard this, all   Mt. xxvii. 23.
cried out: "No, punish him in the Roman
fashion! Stretch him on the cross!" Pilate   21.
heard them out, and said to the chief priests:
"Well, as you will! But you have a custom
at the feast of the Passover to pardon one
condemned malefactor. Well, I have lying
in prison, Barabbas, a murderer and rioter.
Which one of the two must be let free:
Jesus or Barabbas?"

Pilate thus wished to save Jesus; but the
chief priests had so worked upon the people,
that all cried out: "Barabbas, Barabbas!"

And Pilate said: "And what shall be done   22
with Jesus?"

They again cried out: "Roman fashion,—
to the cross, to the cross with him."

Mt. xxvii. 23. And Pilate tried to talk them over. He said:
"Why do you press so hardly on him? He
has done nothing that he should be punished

Jn. xix. 4. with death, and he has done you no harm. I
will set him free, because I find no fault in him."

6. The chief priests and their servants cried
out: "Crucify, crucify him!"

And Pilate said to them: "If so, then take
him and crucify him yourselves. But I see no
fault in him."

7. The chief priests answered: "We ask only
that which our law demands. By our law, he
must be executed for having made himself out
to be Son of God."

8. When Pilate heard this word, he was
troubled, because he did not know what this

9. term "Son of God" meant. And having
returned into the court, Pilate called up Jesus
again, and asked him: "Who are you, and
whence are you?"

But Jesus did not answer.

10. Then Pilate said: "But why do you not
answer me? You surely see that you are in
my power, and that I can crucify you, or set
you free."

11. Jesus answered him: "You have no power.
There is power only from above."

12. Pilate, nevertheless, wished to set Jesus free,

15. and he said to them: "How is it you wish to
crucify your king?"

12. But the Jews said to him: "If you set Jesus
free, you will thereby show that you are a dis-
loyal servant to Cæsar, because he who sets
himself up as king is an enemy to Cæsar.

15. Our king is Cæsar; but crucify this man."

13. And when Pilate heard these words, he
understood that he could now no longer
refuse to execute Jesus.

Then Pilate went out before the Jews, took Mt. xxvii. 24
some water, washed his hands, and said: "I
am not guilty of the blood of this just man."
And the whole people cried out: "Let his 25.
blood be upon us and all our children."

So that the chief priests gained the upper Lk. xxiii. 23.
hand. And Pilate sat in his place of judgment, Jn. xix. 13.
and ordered Jesus to be first flogged. Mt. xxvii. 26.

When they had flogged him, the soldiers, 28,
who had done this, put a crown upon his head 29.
and a rod in his hand, and threw a red cloak
over his back, and fell to reviling him; in
mockery, they bowed down to his feet, and
said: "Hail, king of the Jews!" And others
struck him on the cheeks, over the face, and
spat in his face.

But the chief priests cried: "Crucify him! Jn. xix. 15.
Our king is Cæsar! Crucify him!"

And Pilate bade him be crucified. 16.

Then they stripped Jesus of the red dress, Mt. xxvii. 31.
put on him his own clothing, and bade him
bear the cross to a place called Golgotha, there
to be crucified at once. And he carried his Jn. xix. 18.
cross, and so came to Golgotha. And there
they stretched Jesus on the cross, beside two
other men. These two were at the sides, and
Jesus was in the middle.

When they had crucified Jesus, he said: Lk. xxiii. 34.
"Father! forgive them; they do not know what
they are doing."

And when Jesus was hung on the cross, the 35.
people thronged round him and railed at him.
They came up, wagged their heads at him, and Mk. xv. 29.
said: "So, you wish to destroy the temple of
Jerusalem, and to build it up again in three
days. Well now, save yourself, come down from 30.
the cross!" And the chief priests and leaders 31.
stood there also, and mocked at him, and said:
"He thought to save others, but cannot save
himself. Now show that you are Christ; come 32.

down from the cross, and then we will believe
you. He said that he was the Son of God,
and that God would not forsake him. But how
is it that God has now forsaken him?" And
the people, and the chief priests, and the
soldiers, railed at him, and even one of the
robbers crucified with him, he too railed at
him.

Lk. xxiii. 39. One of the robbers, reviling him, said: "If
you are Christ, save yourself and us."

40. But the other robber heard this and said:
"Do you not fear God? You who are yourself on the cross, do you even rail at the inno-

41. cent? You and I are executed for our deserts,
but this man has done no harm."

42. And, turning to Jesus, this robber said to
him: "Lord, remember me in your kingdom."

43. And Jesus said to him: "Even now you are
blessed with me!"

Mt.xxvii. 46. But at the ninth hour, Jesus, worn out, cried
aloud: "Eloi, Eloi, lama sabachthani!" This
means: "My God, my God! why hast Thou
forsaken me?"

47. And when the people heard this, they began
to say jeeringly: "He is calling the prophet
Elias! Let us see whether Elias will come!"

Jn. xix. 28. Afterward, Jesus cried out: "Let me
drink!"

And a man took a sponge, soaked it in
vinegar, that stood by, and gave it to Jesus on
a reed.

30. Jesus sucked the sponge, and cried out in a
loud voice: "It is finished! Father, I give up

Lk. xxiii. 46. my spirit into your hands!" And, letting his
head fall, he gave up the ghost.

A PROLOGUE

THE UNDERSTANDING OF LIFE

*The proclamation of Christ has replaced the belief in an
external God by the understanding of life*

THE Gospel is the revelation of this truth,
that the first source of everything is the understanding of life itself.   This being so, the
Gospel puts in the place of what men call
" God " a right understanding of life.   With
out this understanding there is no life ; men
only live in so far as they understand life.

Those who do not grasp this, and who deem
that the body is the source of life, shut themselves out from true life ; but those who comprehend that they live, not through the body,
but through the spirit, possess true life.   This
is that true life which Jesus Christ came to
teach to men.   Having conceived that man's
life flows from the understanding, he gave to
men the teaching and example of a life of the
understanding in the body.

Earlier religions were the announcements of
law as to what men ought to do, and not to
do, for the service of God.   The teaching of
Jesus, on the other hand, deals only with the
understanding of life.   No man has ever seen,
and no man can see or know, an external God ;
therefore our life cannot take for its aim the
service of such a God.   Only by adopting for
his supreme principle the inner understanding

of life, having for its source the acknowledgment of God, can man surely travel the way of life.

Mk. I. 1.
Jn. xx. 31.

The announcement of salvation of Jesus Christ, the Son of God. This is the announcement of salvation ; all men who come to know

i. 1. they are sons of God receive true life. The foundation and beginning of all things is the understanding of life. Understanding of life

2. is God. This the announcement of Jesus Christ reveals as the foundation and beginning

3. of everything. All is built upon the understanding of life, without which there can be

4. no living. In this is true life.

5. This understanding is the light of truth. But this light shines amid the darkness, and

9. the darkness is not able to overcome it. The true light has always been in the world, and shines upon all men who come into the world.

10. It has been in the world, and the world existed only because it contained this light; but the

11. world has not adhered to it. This light has appeared in its place, but its place has not retained it.

12. All those who have grasped the understanding of life have received the opportunity of

13. becoming like it through belief in it. Those who have believed that life is in the understanding have become the sons, not of the flesh, but of the understanding.

14. And the understanding of life was united with the flesh in the person of Jesus Christ, and so we were given to know that the offspring of understanding, man in the flesh, is of the same nature as his Father, the original source of life.

15. The teaching of Jesus is the perfect and

16. true faith. In fulfilling the teaching of Jesus, we have understood the new faith which re-

places the old. It was law that Moses gave, Jn.   i. 17.
but we come to understand the true faith
through Jesus Christ.

No man has ever seen God; the Son only,   18.
who is in the Father, has shown us the way
of life.

A SUMMARY

THE UNDERSTANDING OF LIFE IS TO DO GOOD

The announcement of blessedness made by Jesus Christ is an announcement of understanding of life

THE understanding of life is this : The source of life is perfect goodness, and therefore human life is perfectly good in its nature. To understand the source of life, it is necessary to believe that our spirit, the life in man, came from this source. The man, formerly not living, is summoned into life by this, his origin. This source of life appoints blessedness for man, because its own being is blessedness.

To keep in harmony with the source of his life, a man must fix himself upon the one characteristic of this source which is comprehensible to him, and which finds blessedness in doing good. Therefore man's life must be devoted to this blessedness; that is, to doing good from love. But we can find no objects of goodness other than men. All our own bodily desires are out of harmony with this principle of blessedness ; and therefore they, with all the life of the body, must be surrendered to the principle of blessedness, to active love to mankind.

Love to our fellow-men follows from the understanding of life revealed by Jesus Christ. The confirmations of this understanding of life are twofold. One is, that when not accepted, the source of life seems to be an impostor, who gives to men an unsatisfied craving for life and blessedness. The other is, that man feels in his soul that love and goodness toward his fellow-men is the only true, free, eternal life.

The First Epistle of John the Divine

This is the announcement of the understand-   1 Jn. i. 1-3
ing of life through which men have fellowship with the Father of life, and therefore have eternal life.

This is an announcement of blessedness.   4.

The understanding of life is, that God is life   5.
and blessedness, and that in life and blessedness death and evil do not exist.

If we say that we are at one with God, while   6.
we feel we are living in evil and death, then either we are imposing upon ourselves, or we are not doing what we ought to do.

Only by living the same life as His, do we   7.
become at one with Him.

As a teacher of this life, we have Jesus   ii. 1.
Christ, the right-living. He freed us and all   2.
who will, from wrong-living.

The proof that we know the teaching of   3.
Jesus Christ is, that we carry out his commandments. Any one who says he knows the teach-   4.
ing of Jesus Christ, and does not keep his commandments, is a liar, and there is no truth in him. But the man who carries out his   5
commandments has the love of God in him. Only through love can we know that we are at one with God.

He who says he is at one with Jesus Christ,   6.
must also live as Jesus lived.

He who says of himself that he is in life   9-11.
and blessedness, but hates his living brother-man, is not in life and blessedness, but in

death and evil; and he does not know what
he is doing; he is blind, hating the life which
is in himself also.

1 Jn. ii. 15.   To escape this blindness, a man must remember that everything in the world, in the
earthly life, is the desire of the flesh, or vanity,
and that all this is not from God.   And that
16. all this passes away, perishes.   And that only
17. he who does the will of God, which is love,
endures for ever.

23.   Only he who recognizes that his spirit is
the offspring of the Father, is united with the
24. Father.   Therefore remain in the knowledge
that you are, in the spirit, sons of the Father,
God, and you will have eternal life.

iii. 1.   God gives us the opportunity of being His
sons, and like Himself.   So that, in this present
2. life, we become His sons.   We do not know
what we are to be, but we know that we
are like Him, and that we are united with
Him.

3.   Confidence in this eternal life rids us of our
mistakes, and purifies us to the Father's purity.
4. For whoever commits sin, violates the will of
God.

5.   Jesus Christ came to teach us the way to
deliverance from sin, and unity with God.
6. Therefore those who become united with
Him can no longer sin.   Only that man will
7. sin who does not know Him.   But he who
8. lives in God, acts righteously; and only he
9. who is not united with God, does unright-
eously.   He who owns his origin from God,
cannot do any falsehood.

10.   Therefore men are of two classes — men of
God, and men who are not of God; men who
know the right and love the brethren, and
men who do not know the right and do not
love the brethren.

11.   For, following the teaching of Jesus Christ,

we cannot refrain from loving one another. Through the teaching of Jesus Christ, we know that we have passed from death to life, because we love the brethren, and that he who does not love his brother is in death. We know that one who does not love his living brother does not love life. And he who does not love life cannot himself possess life.

By this teaching we recognize love, in the fact that life is given to us; and we know, therefore, that we also must give up our life for our brother. So that he who, himself having the means of life, sees his brother in need, and does not yield his own life for his brother's sake, — in him there is no divine love.

We must love, not by words, but by deeds, in truth. And he who so loves has a quiet heart, because he is at one with God.

If our heart is at strife in us, we subdue it to God. For God is higher than the wishes of our hearts. But if there is no strife in our hearts, then we are blessed, and that because we do all we can, the best deeds, and fulfil all that is ordained for us.

And this is ordained for us — to believe that man is the son of God, and to love our brother. Those who do this are united with God, and are risen above the world, because that which is in us is greater, of more consequence, than all the world.

Therefore let us love one another. Love is from God, and every one who loves is the son of God, and knows God. And he who does not love, does not know God. Because God is love.

That God is love, we know because He sent into the world this Spirit, such as He Himself is, and thereby gave us life. We did not exist, and God was under no compulsion, but

1 Jn. iii 14.

15.

16.

17.

18.
19.

20.
21.

22.

23.

iv. 4.

7.

8.

9.

10.

He gave us life and blessedness; therefore
He must love us.

1 Jn. iv. 11-13. No man can perfectly know God. All we
can know of Him is, that He had love toward
us, and because of this love gave us life. And
to be in fellowship with God, we must be like
Him, and do as He does; we must love one
another. If we love one another, God dwells
in us, and we dwell in Him.

16. Having understood the love of God toward
us, we believe that God is love, and that he
17. who loves is united with God. And having
understood this, we do not fear death, because
in this world we become such as God Himself
18. is. Our life becomes love, and is thus freed
from fear and all sufferings.

19. We love, because He loves. And we love
not a God whom no one can love, because no
one sees Him, but our brother-man, whom it is
20. possible to love. He who says he loves God,
and yet hates his brother, is deceiving himself.
Because, if he does not love the brother whom
he sees, how, then, can he love God whom he
21. does not see? For it is ordained to us to love
God in our brother.

v. 3. To love God, is to fulfil His commandments.
And these commandments are not hard for
4. him who, recognizing that his origin is from
5. God, rises above the world. Our faith lifts us
above the world. And our faith in that which
Jesus, the Son of God, taught us, is true. He
has taught us that he lived in the world, not
merely in the way of truth, but by the power
6. of the spirit. And that spirit is in us, and
makes us strong in truth, following out the
teaching.

9. If we believe in what men affirm, why, then,
should we not believe in the spirit that is in
10. ourselves? He who believes in that spirit of
life which is in us, has assurance within him-

self.   And he who does not believe that there
is a spirit from above us, from the Father,
makes God a deceiver.

The spirit in us affirms that our life is eter-   1 Jn.   v. 11.
nal.   He who knows that this spirit is the off-   12.
spring of the Infinite Spirit, and becomes like
Him, has eternal life.   And for him who so   14.
believes, there is no difficulty left in his life,
but everything he desires in the will of the
Father will come to him.

Therefore he who believes himself to be a   18.
son of God, will not live in any deception, but
is free from evil.   Because he knows that this   19.
material world is an illusion, and that in man   20.
himself there is the capacity to know that which
has real existence.   And only the Spirit, the
Son, the offspring of the Father, really exists.

A RECAPITULATION

CHAPTER I

THE SON OF GOD

Man, the son of God, is powerless in the flesh, and free in the spirit

("Our Father")

JESUS in his childhood called God his Father. There arose in Judea, at this time, a prophet named John. John preached the coming of God upon earth. He said that when men should change their lives, when they should treat one another as equals, when they should cease to injure one another, and, instead of so doing, serve one another, then God would appear upon earth, and His kingdom would be established on earth. Jesus, having heard this declaration, withdrew from among men and went into the wild places, to meditate upon the meaning of human life, and upon his relations to that infinite source of all being, called God. And Jesus accepted as his Father that infinite source of being whom John had called God.

After passing days in the wild places without taking food, Jesus began to suffer hunger. Then he thought to himself, "I am the Son of God the Almighty; I ought, then, to be as He is. But now, I wish to eat, and no bread comes for my need; I am not, then, all-powerful." Then he said to himself, "It is true, I cannot make for myself bread out of stones; but I can overcome the want of bread. So that, though not all-powerful in the body, I am all-powerful in the spirit, and I can quell the body; and thus I am the Son of God, not through the flesh, but through the spirit."

Then he said: "But if I am the Son of the Spirit, I can free myself of the body, and do away with it." But to that he answered, "I am born as spirit, embodied in flesh. Such is the will of my Father, and I cannot set myself against His will."

"But if you cannot satisfy the wants of your body, and if you are no better able to free yourself from your body," he went on to himself, "you ought, then, to labor for the body, and to enjoy all the pleasures it gives you."

But to that he answered, "I cannot satisfy the wants of my body any better than I can rid myself of it; but my life is all-powerful, in that it is the spirit of my Father; and it follows that in my body I must serve the spirit, my Father, and labor for Him only! And becoming convinced that man's life is only in the spirit of the Father, Jesus left the wild places, and began to declare his teaching to men. He said that the spirit dwelt in him, that henceforth heaven was opened, that the powers of heaven were brought to men, that for men a free and boundless life was begun, and that all men, however unfortunate in the body, may be happy.

CHAPTER II

LIFE IN THE SPIRIT

Therefore man must work, not for the flesh, but for the spirit

("Which art in heaven")

THE Jews, holding themselves orthodox, worshiped an external God, whom they regarded as Creator and Lord of the Universe. According to their teaching, this external God had made an agreement with them. According to this agreement, he had promised the Jews to help them, and they had promised to worship Him; and the chief condition of the alliance was the keeping of the Sabbath.

But Jesus said: "The Sabbath is a human institution. That man shall live in the spirit, is more important than all religious ceremonies. Like all external forms of religion, the keeping of the Sabbath includes in itself a delusion. It is impossible to do nothing on the Sabbath. Good actions must be done at any time; and if keeping the Sabbath prevents good action, then the Sabbath is an error."

Another condition in this agreement with God, was the avoidance of the society of infidels. As to this, Jesus said: "God asks for no sacrifice to Himself, but only that men should love one another."

Still another condition related to the following of rules about washing and cleansing; as to which, Jesus said: "God demands, not outside cleanliness, but only, pity and love toward men." He taught that all such external ceremonies were harmful, and that the church tradition itself was an evil. The church tradition causes men to neglect the most important acts of love, as, for instance, love to father and mother. Of all external ceremonies, of all the ritual of the old law, which had for object, as was held, the purification of men, Jesus said: "Know all of you, that nothing from outside can defile a man; only what he thinks, and what he does, defiles him."

After this, Jesus went to Jerusalem, a town considered holy, entered the temple, where the orthodox believed that God dwelt, and there taught: "It is useless to offer God sacrifices; man is of more consequence than a temple; and the only duty is, to love one's neighbor, and help him."

And he taught, further: "Men need not worship God in any particular place, but they must worship Him in spirit and in act. The spirit cannot be seen or shown. The spirit is man's consciousness of his sonship to the Infinite Spirit. No temple is needed. The true temple is the society of men united in love." He said: "All external worship of the divine is not only false and injurious, as with the Jews, among whom it caused murder and admitted neglect of parents, but harmful, because one who goes through external ceremonials, thinks himself made righteous, and free from the need of doing what love demands." He said: "Only that man aims at good, and does good, who feels his own imperfection. To do good deeds, a man must think of himself as imperfect. But external acts of worship lead men into the delusion of self-conceit. All external ceremonies are unnecessary, and must be thrown aside. Deeds of love are incompatible with ceremonial performances, and it is impossible to do good in that form. Man is the son of God by the spirit, and therefore must serve the Father in the spirit."

CHAPTER III

THE SOURCE OF LIFE

The life of all men has proceeded from the spirit of the Father

("Hallowed be Thy Name")

JOHN's disciples asked Jesus what was meant by his "Kingdom of God." He said that the Kingdom of God as preached by him was also that preached by John; and that therein every man, however poor, might be blessed.

And Jesus said to the people: "John was the first who preached to men a Kingdom of God which is not of the external world, but is in the soul of man. The orthodox went to hear John, but understood nothing, because they know only those fictions of their own about an external God, which they preach; and they are astonished when no one pays heed to them. But John preached the truth of the Kingdom of God within men, and therefore he did more than them all. He did so much that, since his time, the law and the prophets, and all external forms of divine worship, are superseded. Since he taught, it is made clear that the Kingdom of God is in the soul of man.

"The beginning and the end of all things is in the soul

of man. Every man, in addition to his bodily life, to the fact which he knows as to his conception from a bodily father through a bodily mother, recognizes in himself a free spirit, intelligent, and independent of the body. This very Spirit, infinite, and proceeding from the infinite, is the origin of all, and is what we call God. We know Him only as we recognize Him within us. This Spirit is the source of our life, and must be ranked above everything; and to Him we must live. By making Him the foundation of our life, we gain the true and infinite life.

"The Father-Spirit, who sends this Spirit into men, cannot have sent Him to deceive men, so that, while conscious of Him, they might come to lose Him. This infinite Spirit being in man, He must have been given to the end that men, through Him, might have infinite life. Therefore the man who conceives of this Spirit as his life, has infinite life. The man who does not so conceive, has no true life. Men can of themselves choose life or death. Life,—in the Spirit; death, — in the flesh. The life of the Spirit is goodness, light. The life of the flesh is evil, darkness. To believe in the Spirit means to do good deeds; to disbelieve, means to do evil deeds. Goodness is life; evil is death.

"God, the Creator, external to us, the beginning of all beginnings, we do not know. Our conception of Him can only be this, that He sowed in men the Spirit; sowing, as a sower does, everywhere, not discriminating, over the field; and the seed, falling on good ground, grows, falling on sterile ground, perishes.

"The Spirit alone gives life, and men are responsible for keeping or losing it. To the Spirit, no evil exists. Evil is but an illusion of life. There are only the two conditions, of living and not-living. Thus the world presents itself to every man; and for every man there is in his soul a consciousness of the Kingdom of Heaven. Each one can, by his own free will, enter, or not enter, that Kingdom. To enter, belief in the life of the Spirit is necessary. He who believes in that life of the Spirit, has infinite life."

CHAPTER IV

GOD'S KINGDOM

Therefore the will of the Father is the life and welfare of all men

("Thy kingdom come")

JESUS pitied men because they did not know true blessedness; therefore he taught them.   He said: "Blessed are those who have no property, no position, and who do not care for these; and unhappy are they who seek riches and position.   Because such poor and oppressed people are in the Father's will; but the rich and acknowledged people seek only to make gain from men for this temporary life.   To carry out God's will, one must not fear to be poor and despised, but must rejoice in this, while showing men what true happiness is.

"To carry out the will of the Father, which gives life and welfare, mankind must fulfil five commandments, namely: —

The First Commandment

To do no ill to any one, and to so act as to rouse evil in no one; because from evil comes evil.

The Second Commandment

Not to follow after women, and not to desert the woman with whom a union has once been formed; because desertion and change of wives causes all the world's dissoluteness.

The Third Commandment

To take no oath of any kind; because nothing can be promised, since man is in the Father's power; and oaths when taken, are for bad ends.

The Fourth Commandment

Not to fight against evil, but to suffer wrong, and to give even more than men would exact from us; not to condemn, and not to use the law; because every man is himself full of errors, and cannot guide others. By taking revenge, we only teach others to revenge.

The Fifth Commandment

To make no difference between a fellow-countryman and a foreigner; because all men are children of one father.

"The observance of these five commandments is necessary, not to win praise from men, but for one-self, for one's own welfare; therefore there is no propriety in praying and fasting in sight of men.

"The Father knows all that men need, and there is no necessity to pray for particular things; it is simply needful to seek to be in the Father's will. And this is the will of the Father, that a man shall have no anger toward any other. To keep fasts is not essential, for men may fast merely to win praise from men, and such praise ought to be avoided. It is only necessary carefully to conform to the will of God, and the rest will follow of itself. While caring for the body, care cannot be given to the Kingdom of Heaven. Even though a man does not trouble about food and clothing, he will live on. The Father will give life. The needful thing is, at this present moment, to be in the will of the Father. The Father gives to his children what they need. We must desire only the power of the Spirit, which the Father gives.

"The five commandments mark out the road to the Kingdom of Heaven. This narrow path alone leads to eternal life. False teachers — wolves in the skins of sheep — always try to turn men astray from this road; they must be guarded against. False teachers can always be detected, because they teach evil in the

name of good. If they teach violence and executions,
they are false teachers. By the deeds they teach they
may be known.

"Not that man does the Father's will, who calls on
the name of God ; but he who does good deeds. And
he who fulfils these five commandments will have
secure and true life, of which nothing can deprive
him. But he who does not fulfil them will have an
insecure life; one soon to be taken from him, leaving
him nothing."

The teaching of Jesus filled the people with admira-
tion and joy, because it offered freedom to every one.

The teaching of Christ was the fulfilment of John's
prophecy that God's chosen one should bring light to
men, overcome evil, and restore truth, by kindness,
meekness, and goodness, but not by violence.

CHAPTER V

THE TRUE LIFE

*The fulfilment of the personal will leads to death; the fulfilment of the
Father's will gives the true life*

("Thy will be done")

THE wisdom of life is, the recognition of one's own
life as the offspring of the Father's Spirit. Men set
before themselves the aims of the bodily life, and in
pursuing these aims, they harass themselves and others.

In receiving the doctrine of the spiritual life, and in
subjecting and making less of the body, men will find a
full satisfaction in the life of the Spirit, in that life
which is appointed for them.

Jesus said to his disciples: "The true food of man
is the fulfilment of the will of the Father-Spirit. This
fulfilment is always possible. Our whole life is a gathering of the fruits of the life sown within us by the Father.
Those fruits are the good we are doing among men.

"We ought not to look forward with anxiety for anything. We ought, without ceasing our interest in life, to do good among men."

After this, Jesus happened to be in Jerusalem, where was a bath, beside which lay a sick man, doing nothing but waiting a miracle to cure him. Jesus came, and said to him : " Do not expect a cure by a miracle, but live your life according to your strength, and do not be deluded as to the purpose of life." The invalid obeyed Jesus, got up, and went away.

The orthodox, seeing this, began to reproach Jesus for what he said, and because he had, on the Sabbath, raised an invalid. Jesus said to them : " I did nothing new. I have only the power to act of our common Father, the Spirit. He lives, and gives life to men, and I have done likewise. And to do this is every man's business. Every one is free, and can live, or not live. To live, is to fulfil the will of the Father, which is to do good to others. Not to live, is to fulfil one's own will, not to do good to others. It is in every one's power to do this, or that ; to gain life, or to destroy it.

" The true life of man is like this. A master apportioned to his slaves some valuable property, and told each one to work upon what was given to him. Some worked ; some did not work, but put out of sight what was given to them. The master demanded an account : and to those who worked, he gave yet more than they had ; but from those who did not work, he took away everything."

The portion of valuable property of the master is the Spirit of life in man, who is the son of the Father-Spirit. He who in his life works for the sake of the spirit-life, receives infinite life ; he who does not work, is deprived of what was given to him.

The true life is the common life of humanity, and not the life of the individual. Each one must work for the life of others.

After this, Jesus went to a desert place, and many people followed him. At evening, the disciples came, and said : " How shall we feed all these people ? " Among the gathering were some who had nothing, and

some who had bread and fish. And Jesus said to his
disciples: "Give me all the bread you have." He took
the loaves, and gave bread to his disciples, who gave to
others, who did likewise. So all ate of others' bread,
not consuming all there was, and all were satisfied. And
Jesus said: "Act just in this way. It is not necessary
that each one should get food for himself, but it is needful to do that which the Spirit in man demands, namely,
that each shall share to others what supply there is.
The true food of man is the Spirit of the Father.
Man lives by the Spirit only. Everything in life must
be made subservient to this; for life consists in doing,
not one's own will, but the will of the Father of life.
And that will is, that the perfect life of the Spirit
which is given to men, shall remain in them, and that
all shall cherish the life of the Spirit within them until
the hour of death. The Father, the source of life, is
Spirit. Life consists only in carrying out the will of the
Father; and to carry out that will of the Spirit, one must
surrender the body. The body is the food, the material
for the life of the Spirit. Only in giving up the body
does the Spirit live."

After this, Jesus chose certain disciples, and sent
them everywhere to preach the doctrine of the life of
the Spirit. In sending them, he said: "Preach the
life of the Spirit, and, consistently therewith, renounce
beforehand all fleshly desires, and have nothing of your
own. Be ready for persecution, privation, suffering.
Those who love the life of the body will hate you,
harass and murder you; but do not fear. If you fulfil
the will of the Father, then you possess the life of the
Spirit, of which no one can deprive you."

The disciples went away, and when they returned,
declared that everywhere the teachings of evil were
conquered by them.

Then the orthodox told Jesus that his teaching,
even if it conquered evil, was in itself an evil, because
those who carry it out must of necessity suffer. To
this, Jesus answered: "Evil cannot conquer evil. If
evil is conquered, it can only be by good. Goodness

is the will of the Father-Spirit common to all men. Every man has a knowledge of what benefits himself. If he does similar benefits to others, if he does that which is the will of the Father, then he will do good. Therefore the carrying out of the will of the Father-Spirit results well, even though it be followed with sufferings and deaths of those who fulfil that will."

CHAPTER VI

THE FALSE LIFE

Therefore, in order to receive the true life, man must on earth resign the false life of the flesh, and live by the Spirit

("On earth as in heaven")

To the spiritual life there can be no difference between members of one family and strangers. Jesus said that his mother and his brethren, as such, had no superior claims upon him; only those were near to him who fulfilled the will of the common Father. A man's life and welfare depend, not on family relations, but on the life of the Spirit.

Jesus said: "Blessed are those who retain their understanding of the Father. The man who lives by the Spirit has no home, for, being by the Spirit, he cannot own any special house." And he said that he himself had no fixed abode; that not being needed to enable a man to carry out the will of the Father, which can be done at all times, in all places.

The death of the body cannot be dreadful to a man who gives himself up to the will of the Father, because the life of the Spirit goes on despite the death of the body. Jesus said that he who believes in the life of the Spirit has nothing to fear.

No cares make it impossible for a man to live in his Spirit. When a man said that he would obey the teaching of Christ presently, but that he must first bury his father, Jesus answered: "Only the dead trouble about

burial of the dead; but the living live always in fulfilling the will of the Father." Cares about relations and
family affairs must not hinder the life of the Spirit. He
who troubles about the results to his bodily life from the
fulfilment of the Father's will, does as the plowman
does, who plows, looking not in front, but behind.

Cares for the pleasures of the bodily life, which seem
so important to men, are delusions. The only, the real
business of life, is the making plain of the Father's will,
attention to it, and fulfilment of it. To Martha's reproach, that she alone troubled about the supper, and
that her sister Mary did not help, but listened to his
teaching, Jesus said: "You blame her unjustly. Take
some trouble, yourself, if you need what comes of it, but
let those who do not need pleasures for the body attend
to the one essential business of life."

And Jesus said: "He who desires the true life, which
comes of fulfilling the Father's will, must first of all give
up his own personal desires." He must not only cease
to plan out his life to his own wishes, but he must be
ready at any moment to bear any privations and sufferings. One who seeks to arrange his bodily life to his
own desires, will wreck the true life of fulfilment of the
Father's will.

Most ruinous to the life of the Spirit is the love of
gain, of getting rich. Men forget that, however much
they acquire riches and goods, they may die at any
moment, and their property is not an essential of life.
Death broods over every one of us. Sickness, killing
by men, fatal accidents, may at any minute end life.
Bodily death is the unescapable condition of every
second of life. While one lives, one must regard every
hour of life as a delay granted by the kindness of
some power. This we must remember, and not say that
we do not know it. We know and foresee in regard
to all events of earth and sky, but death, which we
know waits on us every moment, we forget. But unless
we forget death, we cannot yield ourselves to the life
of the body, we cannot build upon it. To follow the
teaching of Christ, one has to count up the advantages

of serving the bodily life, of serving one's own will, and the advantages of fulfilling the Father's will. Only one who clearly takes account of this can be a disciple of Christ. And he who makes the calculation, will not prefer a visionary benefit and a visionary life to the true good and the true life. The true life has been given to men, and men know it, they hear its summons, but, always swept on by the cares of the moment, they are withheld from it. The true life is as though a rich man gave a feast, and summoned the guests. His call to them is the voice of the Spirit of the Father inviting all men to Himself. But of those invited some are busy in commerce, some in the household, some in family affairs, — none come to the feast. Only the poor, such as have no cares of the body, come to the feast, and gain happiness. So men, distracting themselves with cares for the bodily life, are losing the true life. He who cannot, and that altogether, decline the cares and gains of the bodily life, cannot fulfil the Father's will, because one cannot serve oneself a little, and the Father a little.

A man must calculate, whether it is better to serve the body, whether it is possible to arrange his life according to his own will. He must do as one does who would build a house, or who contemplates war. Such an one will reckon whether he has means to finish building, whether he has means to conquer. And upon seeing that he has not, he will not spend for nothing either labor or armies. Otherwise, he fruitlessly wastes, and will be a laughingstock to men. If one could arrange the bodily life to one's own will, then it might be well to serve the body; but as that is impossible, then better sacrifice the body, and serve the Spirit. Otherwise, one will gain neither one thing nor another; the bodily life will not be gained, and the spiritual life will be lost. So that, to fulfil the Father's will, the bodily life must be quite resigned.

The bodily life is involved in the world's false riches, which we are commissioned to manage in such a way as to gain the true and perfect riches.

If a rich man has a manager who knows that, however
he may serve his master, the latter will dismiss him,
leaving him with nothing, this manager will do well if,
during his management of the other's riches, he treats
people well. Then, even though his master dismiss him,
those whom he has benefited will receive him and sus-
tain him. So also must men act as to the bodily life.
The bodily life is that wealth, not one's own, which is
given to one to manage for a time. If men will rightly
use this wealth, which is not their own, then they will
gain true wealth, really their own.

If we do not give up our falsely held riches, then the
true life will not be given to us. The illusory life of
the body, and the life of the spirit, cannot both be
served. One cannot serve property and God. What
is honorable with men, is abomination before God.
Riches are evil before God. A rich man is continually
guilty, in that he eats abundantly and luxuriously, while
at his door the poor starve. And every one knows that
the property which one will not share to others is held
in non-fulfilment of the Father's will.

Once Jesus was approached by an orthodox and rich
ruler, who began to boast that he had fulfilled all the
commandments of the law. Jesus reminded him that
there is a commandment to love others as oneself, and
that this is the Father's will. The ruler said he kept
this also. Then Jesus said to him : "That is not true ;
if you desire to fulfil the Father's will, you would not
have property. A man cannot fulfil the will of the
Father, if he has a fortune of his own, which he does
not give away to others."

And Jesus said to the disciples : "Men think it impossible to live without property, but I tell you, true life is
in the giving up of one's own to others."

A man, Zaccheus by name, heard the teaching of
Jesus, and believed it, and having invited Jesus to his
house, he said to him : "I am giving half my fortune
to the poor, and I will restore four times over to those
whom I may have wronged." And Jesus said : "Here
is a man who fulfils the Father's will ; for the fulfilment

of that will is not a matter of finding an opportunity, but the whole life must go in fulfilment."

Goodness cannot be measured in any way. It is impossible to say who has done more good, and who less. A widow who gives away her last farthing gives more than a rich man who gives thousands. It is also impossible to measure goodness by utility or inutility.

As an instance of how goodness must be shown, take the woman who pitied Jesus, and in her emotion poured upon him many pounds' worth of costly oil. Judas said she had done foolishly, because many people might have been fed on the price. But Judas was a thief; he spoke untruth, and in talking of the worldly value of the oil, he did not consider the poor. Not utility, not value, comes into the question, but the necessity of always, every minute, loving others, and giving up to them one's own.

CHAPTER VII

I AND THE FATHER ARE ONE

The true food of everlasting life is the fulfilment of the Father's will

("Give us our daily bread")

ANSWERING the Jews' demands for proofs of the truth of his teaching, Jesus said: "The truth of my teaching is proved in the fact that I teach, not in my own name, but in the name of the common Father of all men. I teach that which is good in the sight of the Father of all men, and is therefore good for all men.

"Do as I say; fulfil the five commandments, and you will see that the truth is as I say. Fulfilment of these five commandments will drive away all the world's evil; therefore it must be that they are true and right. Clearly, he who teaches, not his own personal will, but the will of Him who sent him, will teach the truth. The Mosaic law teaches the fulfilment of men's own wills, and is therefore full of contradictions; but my teaching is to fulfil the will of the Father, and therefore in it all is harmonious."

The Jews did not understand him, and looked for external proofs as to whether he himself were the Christ written of in the prophecies. On this he said to them: "Do not inquire who I am, whether it is of me your prophecies speak, but attend to my teaching, to what I say of our common Father. It is not necessary to inquire about outside matters, as to whence I come; but my teaching must be followed. He who will follow my teaching will obtain true life. There can be no proofs of my teaching. It is the light itself, and as you cannot illuminate light, so you cannot prove the truth of truth. My teaching is light; he who sees it has light and life, and has no need of proofs. But he who is in darkness must come to the light."

But again the Jews asked him who he was, as to his bodily personality. He said to them: "I am, as I told you from the first, a man, the Son of the Father of life. Only he who will so regard himself (this is the truth I teach), and will fulfil the will of the common Father, only he will cease to be a slave, and become a free man. Because we are slaves only through the error which considers the bodily life as the real life. He who will understand the truth, that life consists only in the fulfilment of the Father's will, only he will become free and immortal. Just as a bond-servant in a master's house is not there for ever, but the son does remain, so the man who lives the life of a slave of the flesh does not remain in life for ever; but he who in spirit fulfils the Father's will, remains in life for ever. To understand me, you must understand that my Father is not that which is your Father, what you call God. Your Father is a God of the flesh; but my Father is the Spirit of life. Your Father, your God, is a God of revenge, a murderer, one who executes men; but my Father gives life. Therefore we are children of different Fathers.

"I am following the truth, and you wish to kill me for that, to please your God. Your God is the devil, the source of evil; and in serving him, you serve the devil

But my teaching is, that we are the sons of the Father of life, and that he who believes in my teaching shall not see death."

The Jews asked : " How can a man not die, when all the most God-pleasing men, even Abraham, are dead ? How, then, can you say that you, and those that believe your teaching, will not die ? " To this Jesus answered : " I speak not by my own authority. I speak of the one source of life, whom you call God, and who is in men. This source I know, I cannot help knowing, and I know His will, and I fulfil it ; and of this source of life I say, that it was, and is, and shall be, being deathless."

The demand for proof of Jesus' teaching is like a demand made upon a once-blind man, to give proofs of how and why he sees light. The blind man whose sight was restored, still the same man he was before, can only say, he was blind, but now sees. Just this, and nothing else, can one answer who formerly did not understand the meaning of life, but now does understand. Such a man will say that he did not, before, know the true good in life, but now he knows. The once-blind man, when told he is cured not according to rule, and that he who cured him is the evil-doer, and that he must be cured in another way, can only reply, that he knows nothing as to the correctness of the manner of cure, or as to the faultiness of his healer, or as to their being a better way of cure, but that he knows only, he was blind, and now sees. And just so, he who grasps the meaning of this doctrine, that the true good is to fulfil the Father's will, can say nothing as to the regularity of the teaching, or as to the possibility of gaining something better. He will say : " Formerly I did not see the meaning of life ; now I see. I know no more."

And Jesus said : " My teaching is the awakening of the life which has so far slept ; he who will believe my teaching, shall awaken to eternal life, and continue to live after death. My teaching is not proved in any way, except that men give themselves up to it, because it alone has the promise of life for men.

"Sheep follow the shepherd, who gives them food and life; and in the same way, men accept my teaching because it gives life to all. And as the sheep do not follow the thief who climbs over into the fold, but throw themselves aside from him, so men, also, cannot accept the doctrines which teach violence and putting-to-death.

" My teaching is a door to the sheep, and all who will follow me shall find true life. As those only are good shepherds who own and like the sheep, and devote their lives to them, while the mere hirelings, who have no liking for sheep, are bad shepherds; so, also, only that teacher is true who does not look after himself, and he is bad who cares only about himself. My teaching is, that a man shall not look after himself, but shall yield up the life of the body for the life of the spirit. This I teach and fulfil."

Still the Jews did not understand, and persisted in looking for proofs as to whether or not Jesus was the Christ, to determine whether they should believe in him or not. They said: "Do not torment us, but tell us frankly, are you the Christ, or not?" Then Jesus answered them : "Belief must be given, not to words, but to deeds. By the deeds I teach you may know whether I teach truth or not. Do as I do, and do not trifle over words. Fulfil the will of the Father, and then you will all join with me and with the Father, because I am a Son of Man, and at one with the Father. And I am that which you call God, and I call Father. God and I are one. Even in your own writings it is said, that God said to men, 'You are gods.' Every one, by his spirit, is son of this Father. And if a man lives fulfilling the will of the Father, then he becomes at one with the Father. If I fulfil the will, the Father is in me, and I am in the Father."

After this, Jesus asked the disciples how they under-stood his teaching as to the Son of Man. Simon Peter answered him : "Your teaching is that you are the Son of the God of life; that God is the life of the spirit in man." And Jesus said to him : "Not only I am a son, but all men are; and this is revealed to men, not by me, but by the common Father of men. Upon this knowledge is based the true life of man. To this life there is no death."

CHAPTER VIII

LIFE IS NOT TEMPORAL

Therefore true life is to be lived in the present

("This day")

DEALING with the disciples' question as to the recompense for surrendering the life of the body, Jesus said: "To him who enters into the reality of this teaching, no further recompense can be given; because, first, when a man yields up friends and goods for the sake of this teaching, he gains a hundred times more friends and goods; and second, a man who seeks such recompense wants to have something over and above others, which is entirely contrary to the fulfilment of the Father's will." In the Kingdom of Heaven there is neither great nor small; all are equal. Those who look for something extra as reward for their goodness, are like the laborers who claimed a greater payment than that for which they had agreed with their employer; merely because, in their opinion, they were more deserving than other laborers. There are no rewards, punishments, degradations, or exaltations, for him who understands this teaching. No one can be higher or lower, more or less important, than another, according to the teaching of Jesus.

All can equally fulfil the Father's will. Therefore, in so doing, no one becomes superior, truer, or better, than another.

Kings and those who serve them, they only are measured by such standards. By my teaching, said Jesus, there can be no superior rank, because he who would excel must serve everybody; for the teaching is, that life is given to man, not that others may serve him but that he may give his whole life to serve others; but he who will not do this, but seeks to exalt himself, shall fall lower than he was.

To get rid of all ideas of rewards and of one's elevation, the meaning, purpose, of life must be understood. That lies in fulfilling the will of the Father; and the will of the Father is, that that which He gave shall be returned to Him. As a shepherd leaves his flock, and goes to look for the lost sheep, as a woman will search everywhere to find a lost penny, so also the Father's continual work is manifested to us in His drawing to Himself that which pertains to Him.

We must understand the true life, what it is. The true life is brought to light always in the lost being brought back to where they belong, in the awakening of those who slept. People who have the true life, who are restored to the source of their being, cannot, like worldly men, take account of others as better or worse; but, being sharers of the Father's life, they can take delight only in the return of the lost to their Father. If a son, who has gone astray and left his father, should repent, and return, how then could the other sons of the same father grudge at the father's joy, or themselves not rejoice at the brother's return?

To lead us to believe the teaching, and to alter one's way of living, and fulfil the teaching, we need, not external proofs, not promises of reward, but a clear understanding of what the true life is. If men think they are complete masters of their own lives, and that life is given them for bodily enjoyment, then clearly, any sacrifice made for another will seem to them an act worthy of reward, and without such payment they will yield nothing. A man demands rents from tenants who have forgotten that their ground is theirs on condition that they give up the fruits to the owner; and when he demands the rent again and again, they seek to kill him. So with the men who think themselves masters of their own lives, not discerning that life is given by true understanding; men who demand the fulfilment of their own wills.

Both belief and action are necessary, to learn that a man can do nothing of himself, and if he give up his bodily life to serve goodness, he deserves neither thanks nor reward. We must understand that, in doing good, a man only does his duty, does what he must necessarily do. Only by so understanding his life, can a man have faith to enable him to do deeds of true goodness.

Precisely in such an understanding of life, the Kingdom of Heaven consists. This Kingdom is invisible; it cannot be pointed out as identified with this or that place. The Kingdom of Heaven is in the human understanding. The whole society of the world goes on living as of old; men eat, drink, marry, trade, die, and along with this, in the souls of men, lives the Kingdom of Heaven. It is the understanding of life, growing from itself, like a tree in the spring.

The true life of the fulfilment of the Father's will is not in the life of the past, or of the future, but it is the life of now, the life which all must live at this instant of time. Therefore one must never relax the true life in them. Men are set to watch over life, not of the past or the future, but the life now being lived; and in that, to fulfil the will of the Father of all men. If they let this life escape them, by not fulfilling the Father's will, then they will not receive it back again; just as a watchman, set upon a night-long watch, does not perform his duty if he fall asleep even for a moment; for in this moment a thief may come.

Therefore a man must concentrate his strength in the present hour, for in this hour only can he fulfil the Father's will. And that will is life and blessing for all men. Only those live who are doing good. Good done to men, now, in this hour, is life, life which unites us with the common Father.

CHAPTER IX

TEMPTATIONS

The illusions of temporal life conceal from men the true life in the present

("𝔉𝔬𝔯𝔤𝔦𝔟𝔢 𝔲𝔰 𝔬𝔲𝔯 𝔡𝔢𝔟𝔱𝔰 𝔞𝔰 𝔴𝔢 𝔣𝔬𝔯𝔤𝔦𝔟𝔢 𝔬𝔲𝔯 𝔡𝔢𝔟𝔱𝔬𝔯𝔰")

MAN is born with knowledge of the true life of ful-filment of the Father's will.   Children live by that knowledge; through them we may see what the Father's will is.   To understand the teaching of Jesus, one must understand the life of children, and be like them.

Children always live in the Father's will, not breaking the five commandments.   They would not come to break them if their elders did not mislead them.   In misleading children to break those commandments, men ruin the children.   In misleading them, men are doing as they would do by fastening a millstone to a man's neck and throwing him into the water.

If there were no temptations, the world would be happy.   The world is unhappy by them only.   These temptations are wrong-doing which men enact for imaginary gain to the life in time.   Temptations ruin men; therefore it is necessary to give up everything rather than fall into temptation.

Temptation against the first commandment leads men to consider themselves in the right against others, and others as in the wrong, debtors to them.   To avoid this temptation, men must remember that all men are always infinitely in debt to the Father, and they can only clear themselves of this debt by forgiving their brother-men.

Therefore men must overlook injuries, and not be de-terred though the offender again and again injure them. However many times a man may be injured, he must forgive, and still forgive, not remembering the wrong. For the Kingdom of Heaven is forgiveness.

If we do not forgive, we are doing as the debtor did. This debtor, greatly owing, came to him in whose power he was, and began to ask for mercy.   The other forgave him all. The debtor went away, and began himself to squeeze a debtor, who owed him but a little. Now, to gain life, we must fulfil the Father's will. And we pray the Father to forgive us, that we have not duly fulfilled his will, and we hope to be forgiven. What, then, are we doing, if we do not ourselves forgive? We are doing to others what we dread for ourselves.

The will of the Father is well-being, and evil is that which separates us from the Father. Why, then, should we not strive to quench evil right away, when evil ruins us, and takes our life?

Temptation against the second commandment is, to think that woman is created for bodily pleasure, and that in leaving one woman and taking another, heightened pleasure is gained. To avoid this temptation, we must remember that the Father's will is, not that man should amuse himself with woman's charms, but that every man, with his wife, should be one body. The Father's will is, for every man, one wife; for every wife, one husband. If one man keep to one wife, then there is wife or husband for each one who needs. Therefore he who changes the woman he lives with deprives her of a husband, and tempts some other man to leave his wife and take the deserted one. A man may do without a wife, but he must not have more than one, because if he does, he goes against the will of the Father, which is, that one man unite with one woman.

Temptation against the third commandment is, for men to create, for the protection of the temporal life, authoritative powers, and to demand from each other oaths, pledges, to do the deeds those powers demand.

To avoid this temptation, men must remember that they are not indebted for their life to any power but God. The claims of authority must be regarded as violence; and, following the commandment regarding the non-resistance of evil, men must yield what the authorities demand, namely, their goods and labor; but they cannot, either by oaths or promises, pledge their conduct. Oaths, being imposed, make men bad. He who recognizes life in the will of the Father cannot bind his actions by pledges; because for such a man there is nothing more sacred than his own life.

Temptation against the fourth commandment is, for men to hold that, by giving themselves up to animosity and revenge, they can exterminate evil from among themselves. If a man injure another, men think he should be punished, and that justice lies in human judgments. To be free from this temptation, we must remember that men are called, not to judge, but to save each other. To judge of another's injustice is impossible for men, as they themselves are full of wickedness. The only thing open to them is to teach others by example of goodness, forgiveness, and purity.

Temptation against the fifth commandment is, for man to think there is a difference between one's own countrymen and men of other nations; and that it is therefore necessary to make defense against other nations, and to injure them. To avoid this temptation, it is necessary to know that all the commandments are summed up in this one, of fulfilling the will of the Father who gives life and well-being to all men; and therefore it is necessary to do good to all men, without distinction. Even though others still make such distinctions, and though nations who look on each other as aliens are at war, nevertheless, everybody who would fulfil the Father's will must do good to all men, even to those who belong to another nation which is at war.

To avoid falling into any delusions of men, we must not think about bodily affairs, but about spiritual. To him who has understood that life consists in being, at this moment, in the Father's will, neither deprivations, nor suffering, nor death can be dreadful. Only he obtains true life who is, at every moment, ready to give up his bodily life in order to fulfil the Father's will.

And that all may understand the true life to be one in which there is no death, Jesus said: " Eternal life must not be understood to be like this present life. For the true life in the Father's will, there is neither space nor time. Those who are awakened to the true life, live in the will of the Father, for which there is no space nor time ; and they live with the Father.   Though they die to us, they live to God.   Therefore one commandment includes in itself all others ; the commandment, namely, to love, with all our strength, the source of life ; and consequently to love all men, each of whom bears in himself this same original."

And Jesus said : " This source of life is that very Christ which you await.   The comprehension of this source of life, which knows no distinction of persons, no time, no place, is the Son of Man which I teach.   Anything which hides this source of life from men is temptation.   There is the temptation of the scribes, bookmen, and of the materialists ; do not yield thereto.   There are the temptations of authority ; do not yield thereto.   And there is the most terrible temptation, from the teachers of religion who call themselves orthodox.   Beware of this last more than of all others ; because just they, these self-ordained teachers, by inventing the worship of a false God, decoy you from the true God.   They, instead of serving the Father of life by deeds, substitute words, and they teach words, while they themselves do nothing.   Therefore you can learn nothing from them but words.   But the Father requires deeds, not words.   And they have nothing to teach, because they themselves know nothing ; but for their own gain they must parade as teachers.   But you know that no man can be the teacher of another.   There is one teacher for all — the Lord of life — understanding.   And these self-assuming teachers, thinking to teach others, deprive themselves of true life, and prevent others from the understanding of it.   They teach that their God will be pleased with external ceremonies ; and they think they can bring men to serve religion by vows.   They are concerned with appearances only.   An outward assumption of religion suffices them, but they do not care what is in the hearts of men.   Therefore they are like elaborate coffins, very nice outside, but within full of repulsiveness. They give honor, in words, to saints and martyrs, but they are themselves just the very men who have murdered and tortured in the past, and who murder and tor-

ture the saints of to-day. By them come all the world's
temptations; because, under the guise of good, they
teach evil. The temptation they create is the root of all
others, because they defile that which is most sacred.
For a long time yet they will not be changed, but will
continue their deceptions, and increase evil in the world.
But there shall come a time when all the temples will be
ruined, with all the external God-worship; when all men
will understand, and unite in love, to serve the one Father
of life, by fulfilling His will."

CHAPTER X

THE WARFARE WITH TEMPTATION

*Therefore, not to fall by temptation, we must, at every moment of life, be
at one with the Father*

("Lead us not into temptation")

THE Jews saw that the teaching of Jesus would destroy their state, religion, and nationality, and at the
same time they saw they could not controvert him; so
they decided to kill him. His innocence and justness
stood in their way, but the high priest Caiaphas discovered a reason for killing Jesus, though innocent. Caiaphas said: "We need not consider whether this man
is just or unjust; we have to determine whether our
Jewish people shall remain a separate nation, or whether
we shall be broken up and dispersed: the nation will
perish, and the people be scattered, if we leave this
man alone, and do not put him to death." This argu-
ment settled the matter, and the orthodox sentenced
Jesus to death. They instructed the people to seize
upon him as soon as he might appear in Jerusalem.

Jesus, although he knew about this, nevertheless, on
the feast of the Passover, came to Jerusalem. His disciples entreated him not to do so; but he said: "What
these orthodox can do to me, and all that other men can
do, cannot alter the truth for me. If I have the light,
I know where I am, and which way I am going. Only

he who does not know the truth can fear anything, or can doubt anything. Only he who cannot see, stumbles." And he went to Jerusalem, stopping on the way at Bethany.

When he left Bethany, and went to Jerusalem, crowds of people met and followed him. This still more convinced the orthodox of the need to kill him. They only wanted an opportunity to seize him. He knew also that the lightest incautious word from him at that time, spoken against the law, would be a reason for his execution; but notwithstanding this, he entered the temple, and declared again that the worship of the Jews, with their sacrifices and libations, was false, and he declared his teaching. But his teaching, based on the prophets, was such that the orthodox could not yet find a palpable breach of the law which would justify them in putting him to death; the more so that the greater part of the lower class was with Jesus.

At the feast were certain heathen, who, having heard of the teaching of Jesus, wished to talk with him about it. The disciples, hearing of this, were afraid, fearing lest Jesus, in talking with them, should betray himself, and excite the people. At first they would not bring Jesus and these heathen together; but afterward they resolved to tell him these men wanted to see him. Hearing this, Jesus was disturbed. He well knew that his speech to the heathen would clearly show his antagonism to the whole Jewish law, would turn the crowd from him, and would give the orthodox a reason to accuse him of being in league with the hated heathen. Jesus became disturbed, knowing this; but he also knew that his mission was to make clear to men, the children of one Father, their real unity, despite differences of religion. He knew that the step he was about to take would end his bodily life, for the sake of giving birth to spiritual results. He said: "He who holds fast to the bodily life is deprived of the true one; and he who is not careful for the bodily life obtains the true life. I am troubled by what is before me, but I have only lived that I might reach this hour; how, then, can I fail to now do what I must do? So let the Father's will be shown through me now."

And turning to the people, heathen and Jews, Jesus declared openly what he had only privately told to Nicodemus. He said: "Men's lives, with all their various religions and organized powers, must be wholly changed. All power and authority must disappear. It is only necessary to understand the nature of man as the son of the Father of life, and this understanding abolishes all division among men, and all ruling power, and makes men one."

The Jews said: "You wholly destroy our religion. Our law looks to the Christ, but you speak only of the Son of Man, and say that he must be set up. What do you mean?" He answered them: "To set up the Son of Man means to live by the light of the understanding which is in men, to follow this light into more light. I teach no new faith, only that which every one may know within himself. Every man knows he has life, given to him and to all men by the Father of life. My teaching is only this, that man must live the life given by the Father to all."

Many of the humbler kind of people believed Jesus. But the notable and official classes disbelieved; because they did not want to consider the universal basis of what he said, but only its immediate and temporary bearings. They saw that he turned the people from themselves, and they wished to kill him; but they were afraid to seize him openly, and did not seek to do so in Jerusalem and in the daytime, but secretly elsewhere.

And one of the twelve disciples, Judas Iscariot, approached the authorities, and him they bribed to take their emissaries to Jesus when he should be away from the people. Judas promised this, and went again to Jesus, awaiting a suitable opportunity to betray him.

On the first day of the feast, Jesus and his disciples kept the Passover. And Judas, thinking Jesus was not aware of his treachery, was with them. But Jesus knew Judas had sold him. And as they all sat at table, Jesus took bread, broke it in twelve pieces, and gave a piece to each disciple, including Judas with the rest. And not mentioning any name, he said: "Take, eat my body." Then he took the cup with the wine, passed it to them, for them all, including Judas, to drink from, and said: "One of you will shed my blood. Drink my blood."

Afterward Jesus got up, and began to wash the feet of all his disciples, including Judas. And having finished, he said: "I know that one of you will betray me to my death, and shed my blood; but him I have fed, and given to drink, and washed his feet. I have done this to show you how you must act toward those who do you harm. If you will act in this way, you shall be blest." And the disciples went on to ask who the betrayer was. But Jesus did not give his name, so that they might not turn on him. And when it had grown dark, Jesus showed that it was Judas, and at the same time told him to go away. Judas got up from the table and went off, no one hindering him.

Then Jesus said: "This is the meaning of setting up the Son of Man. To set up the Son of Man is to be like the Father, good; and that, not only to those who love us, but to all men, even to those who do us harm. And therefore do not argue over my teaching, do not pick it to pieces as the orthodox did, but do as I have done; do as I have done under your eyes. This one commandment I give you: Love men. My whole teaching is, to love men always, and to the last."

After this, fear came over Jesus, and he went in the dark with his disciples to a garden, to be out of the way. While walking, he said to them: "You are all wavering and timid; if they move to take me, you will all run away." To this, Peter said: "No, I will never leave you; I will defend you even to death." And all the disciples said so. Then Jesus said: "If that be the case, then get ready for defense; take provision, because we must hide, take weapons, to fight for ourselves." The disciples said they had two swords.

When Jesus heard this about the swords, anguish came over him. And going to a vacant place, he be-

gan to pray, and entreated his disciples to do the same.
But the disciples did not understand his state of mind.
Jesus said: "My Father, the Spirit, end in me this
struggle with temptation. Strengthen me to the fulfilment of Thy will. I do not want my own way. I do
not want to defend my bodily life. I want to do Thy
will, in not resisting evil."

The disciples still did not understand. And he said
to them: "Do not consider the concerns of the body,
but try to rise into the spirit; strength is in the spirit,
but the flesh is powerless." And a second time he
said: "My Father, if suffering must be, then let it come.
But even in suffering, I want one thing only: that not
my will shall be fulfilled, but thine." The disciples
did not understand. And again he struggled with the
temptation; and at last conquered it. Coming to the
disciples, he said: "It is settled now; you can be at
rest. I shall not fight, but shall surrender myself into
the hands of the men of this world."

CHAPTER XI

THE FAREWELL DISCOURSE

*The self-life is an illusion which comes through the flesh, an evil. The
true life is the life common to all men*

("Deliver us from evil")

JESUS, finding himself prepared for death, went to give
himself up. Peter stopped him, and asked: "Where are
you going?" Jesus answered: "I am going where you
cannot go. I am ready for death, and you are not yet
ready." Peter said: "No, I am even now ready to sacrifice my life for thee." Jesus said to him: "A man
cannot promise anything."

And he said to all his disciples: "I know death is
before me, but I believe in the life of the Father, and
therefore am not afraid of it. Do not be distressed over

my death, but believe in the real God, in the Father of life, and then my death will not seem dreadful to you. If I am united with the Father of life, then I cannot be deprived of life. It is true, I do not tell you what and where my life will be, after death, but I point out to you the way to true life. My teaching does not reveal what that life is to be, but it reveals the only true way of life. That is, to be in unity with the Father. The Father is the source of life. My teaching is, that man shall live in the will of the Father, and fulfil His will for the life and well-being of all men.

"Your teacher, when I am gone, will be your knowledge of the truth. In fulfilling my teaching, you will always feel that you are in the truth, that the Father is in you, and you are in the Father. And knowing in yourselves the Father of life, you will experience a peace of which nothing will deprive you. And therefore, if you know the truth and live in it, neither my death nor your own can trouble you.

"Men think of themselves as separate beings, each with his own power of will in life; but this is only an illusion. The only true life is that which recognizes the Father's will as the source of life. My teaching reveals this oneness of life, and represents life, not as separate shoots, but as one tree, on which all the shoots grow. Only he who lives in the Father's will, like a shoot of a tree, only he lives; and he who wishes to live by his own will, dies away like a torn-off shoot.

"The Father gave me life to do good, and I have taught you to live to do good. If you will fulfil my commandment, you will be blessed. The commandment which sums up my whole teaching is no more than this, that all men shall love one another. And love is to sacrifice one's own bodily life for another's sake. Love has no other definition. In fulfilling my commandment of love, you will not fulfil it like slaves, who follow the orders of a master without understanding them; but you will live as free men, as I am, because I have made clear to you the purpose of life, which follows from the knowledge of the Father of life. You have adopted my teaching, not from accidental choice, but because it is the only truth by which men are made free.

"The teaching of the world is to do evil to men; but I teach that men love each other. Therefore the world will despise you, as it has despised me. The world does not understand my teaching, and therefore will persecute you, and do you evil, thinking thereby to serve God. Do not be astonished at this; you must understand that it is necessarily so. The world, not understanding the true God, must persecute you; but you must affirm the truth.

"You grieve because they will kill me; but they kill me for declaring the truth. And therefore my death is necessary for the declaration of the truth. My death, in facing which I do not go back from the truth, will strengthen you, and you will understand the nature of untruth and of truth. You will understand that untruth lies in men's belief in the bodily life, and their disbelief in the life of the spirit; that truth consists in unity with the Father, from which results the victory of the spirit over the flesh.

"Even when I shall not be with you in the bodily life, my spirit will be with you. But you, like all men, will not always feel within you the power of the spirit. Sometimes you will relax and lose strength of spirit; and you will fall into temptation; and at times you will again awaken to the true life. Hours of bondage to the body will come upon you, but for a time only; you will suffer, and again be restored to the spirit, like a woman who suffers birth-pangs, and then has joy because she has brought a human being into the world. So will your experience be, when, after falling under the power of the body, you rise again by the spirit. You will then feel such joy, that nothing will be left for you to desire. Know this, then, beforehand; and in spite of persecution, in spite of internal struggle and casting down of spirit, know that the spirit lives in you, and that the only true God is the knowledge of the Father's will, as I have revealed it."

And addressing the Father, the Spirit, Jesus said:

"I have done that which Thou hast commanded me; I have revealed to men that Thou art the source of everything. And they have understood me. I have taught them that they all come from the source of infinite life, and therefore they are all one; and that as the Father is in me, and I am in the Father, so they, too, are one with me and the Father. I have revealed to them also, that, like Thee, who in love hast sent them into the world, they, too, shall with love live in the world."

CHAPTER XII

THE VICTORY OF THE SPIRIT OVER THE FLESH

Therefore, for him who lives, not the self-life, but a common life in the will of the Father, there is no death. Bodily death is for him union with the Father

("Thine is the kingdom, power, and glory")

WHEN Jesus had ended his discourse to the disciples, he rose, and, instead of running away or defending himself, he went on the way to meet Judas, who was bringing soldiers to take him. Jesus came to Judas, and asked him why he had come. But Judas did not answer, and a crowd of soldiers came round Jesus. Peter threw himself forward to defend his teacher, and, drawing his sword, began to fight. But Jesus stopped him, and said to him, that he who fights with a sword must himself perish with the sword, and ordered him to put up the sword. Then Jesus said to those who had come to take him: "I have up to now gone about among you alone, without fear, and I do not fear now. Do as you choose."

And while all the disciples ran away, Jesus was left alone. The officer of the soldiers ordered Jesus to be bound, and led before Annas. This Annas was a former high priest, and lived in the same house with Caiaphas, who was then high priest. Caiaphas it was who provided the reason upon which they decided to kill Jesus; namely, that if he were not killed the nation would disappear.

Jesus, feeling himself to be in the will of the Father, was ready for death, and did not resist when they took him, and was not afraid when they led him away. But the very Peter who had just promised Jesus that he would not renounce him, but would die for him, this same Peter who wished to protect him,—now, when he saw that they were taking Jesus for execution, and being met with the door-keeper's question, Whether he was not with Jesus? gave up, and deserted him. It was only afterward that, hearing the cock crow, Peter brought to mind all that Jesus had said. Then he understood that there are two temptations of the flesh, fear and fighting; and that it was with these that Jesus struggled when he prayed in the garden, and asked the disciples to pray. And now he, Peter, had fallen before both these temptations of the flesh, of which Jesus had forewarned him; he had wished to fight against evil, and to defend the truth, he had been about to strike and to do evil himself; and now he could not endure the fear of bodily suffering, and had renounced his teacher. Jesus had yielded neither to the temptation to fight, when the disciples got ready two swords for his defense, nor to the temptation to fear before the men of Jerusalem, first, in the case of the heathen, and now before the soldiers, who had bound him and led him to trial.

Jesus was taken before Caiaphas. Caiaphas began to question him about his teaching. But knowing that Caiaphas was examining him, not to find out what his teaching was, but only to convict him, Jesus did not answer, but said: "I have concealed nothing, and now conceal nothing. If you wish to know what my teaching is, ask those who heard and understood it." For saying this, the high priest's servant struck Jesus in the face, and Jesus asked him why he so beat him. But the man did not answer him, and the high priest continued the trial. Witnesses were brought, who deposed that Jesus had boasted that he made an end of the Jewish religion. And the high priest interrogated Jesus; who, seeing they did not examine him to learn anything, but only to make a show of a judicial trial, answered nothing.

Then a priest asked him : " Tell me, are you the Christ, the Son of God ? " Jesus said : " Yes, I am the Christ, the Son of God ; and now, in torturing me, you will see how a Son of Man is like to God." And the priest was glad to hear these words, and said to the other judges : " Are not these words enough to condemn him ? " And the judges said : " That is enough ; we sentence him to death." And when they said that, the people threw themselves upon Jesus, and began to beat him, to spit in his face, and insult him. He was silent.

The Jews had no power to punish men with death, and for that needed permission from the Roman governor. Therefore, having condemned Jesus in their court, and having subjected him to ignominy, they took him to the Roman governor, Pilate, that he might execute him. Pilate asked why they wished to kill Jesus. They said, because he was a criminal. Pilate said that if he was so, they must judge him by their own law. They said : " We want you to put him to death, because he is guilty before the Roman Cæsar ; he is a rebel, he agitates the people, he forbids payment of taxes to Cæsar, and calls himself the Jewish king."

Pilate summoned Jesus before him, and said : " What is the meaning of this ; are you the Jewish king ? "

Jesus said : " Do you really wish to know what my kingdom means, or are you only asking for form's sake ? "

Pilate answered : " I am not a Jew, and it is the same to me whether you are the Jewish king or not ; but I ask you, who are you, and why do they call you king ? "

Jesus said : " They say truly, that I call myself a king. I am indeed a king, but my kingdom is not of earth, but of heaven. The kings of the earth war and fight, and have armies ; but as for me, — you see they have bound and beaten me, and I did not resist. I am king from heaven : my power is of the spirit."

Pilate said : " Then it is indeed true that you think yourself a king ? "

Jesus answered: "You know this yourself. Every one who lives by the spirit is free. I live by this only, and I only teach by showing men the truth, that they are free by the spirit."

Pilate said: "You teach the truth, but nobody knows what truth is, and every one has his own truth."

And having said this, he turned his back on Jesus, and went again to the Jews. Coming out to them, he said: "I find nothing criminal in this man. Why, then, put him to death?"

The priests answered: "He ought to be put to death, because he incites the people."

Then Pilate began to examine Jesus before the priests; but Jesus, seeing it was only a mock inquiry, answered nothing. Then Pilate said: "I alone cannot condemn him; take him to Herod."

At Herod's tribunal, Jesus again answered nothing to the accusations of the priests; and Herod, thinking Jesus to be a common fellow, ordered him, for mockery, to be dressed in red clothes, and sent back to Pilate.

Pilate pitied Jesus, and began to entreat the priests to forgive him, if only on account of the feast. But the priests did not consent, and all — the people with them — cried out to crucify Christ. Pilate tried a second time to persuade them to let Jesus go; but priests and people cried out that he must be executed. They said: "He is guilty of calling himself the Son of God." Pilate again summoned Jesus, and asked him what he meant by calling himself the Son of God. Jesus answered nothing.

Then Pilate said: "Why do you not answer me, seeing that I have power to execute you or to set you free?"

Jesus answered: "You have no authority over me; authority only comes from on high."

And Pilate a third time began to persuade the Jews to set Jesus free. But they said to him: "If you will not execute this man, whom we have exposed as an enemy to Cæsar, then you yourself are not a friend, but an enemy, to Cæsar."

And hearing these words, Pilate gave way, and ordered the execution of Jesus. They first stripped him and flogged him; then they dressed him again in a ridiculous way. And they beat him, mocked him, and insulted him. Then they caused him to carry the cross, and led him to the place of execution, where they crucified him.

And as Jesus hung on the cross, the whole populace mocked him. But to this mockery Jesus answered: "Father! do not call them to account; they do not know what they are doing." And then, as he was now drawing near death, he said: "Father! I yield my spirit into Thy care."

And bowing his head, he breathed his last.